Good Evans!

The best of
From the Welsh Borders

Farming
Press

First published 2000

Copyright © Roger Evans

1 3 5 7 9 10 8 6 4 2

ISBN 0 85236 558 6

A catalogue record for this book is available
from the British Library.

Published by Farming Press,
United Business Media, Sovereign House,
Sovereign Way, Tonbridge, Kent TN9 1RW,
United Kingdom

Background cover photograph © Guy Edwardes
Printed & bound in UK by Lavenham Press, Suffolk

CONTENTS

FOREWORD

Having these old issues from *Dairy Farmer* to look at is as near as I shall ever get to keeping a diary. I can still remember how I agonised over the first contribution and when it was despatched, thinking to myself, well at least me and my mam will read it. A reminder too that I was actually voted into the role. The editor had a lot of applicants for the vacancy and so he conducted a poll. I won quite easily, I had twice as many votes as anyone else, I had 12 and two of those were me and my mother!

So many reminders of things we agonised over at the time – should we use continental beef bulls, Holstein bulls, brucellosis, milk quotas and more recently the demise of the MMB. Painful reminders too, our own trauma with abortion at the end of the 70s. Sixty cows aborted out of an eighty-cow herd in twenty months. We think now that it was BVD. No one knew what it was at the time. My overdraft went through the roof and I tried to milk my way out of trouble, 90 cows, 3x a day. Then along came quotas, that year we sold nearly 700,000 litres and ended up with a quota of 400,000.

What I have always tried to do is not take myself too seriously, and to share with you the things that go wrong and the funny things that happen. Dairy farmers have always related to chat and fortunately the funny things keep on coming.

Roger Evans
September 2000

The Seventies

April 1977

By the time that this, my first contribution to *Cowmen Comment*, appears in print, I sincerely hope that spring will have arrived and that we will have the cows out at grass. If there is one single thing that makes dairy farming worthwhile, it must surely be the pleasure of getting the cows out after a long winter.

The arrival of spring will be particularly welcome this year as the winter has not been without its difficulties. We had a lot of trouble keeping the cubicle beds clean. The cows seemed very loose this winter. This, coupled with the fact that 19 of the 60 in the herd were heifers – which tend to lie very short or to back in – made some milkings very unpleasant.

We have always prided ourselves on the low incidence of mastitis in our herd but this last winter has had its problems. We had a group of about six older animals which I had decided to cull next autumn but which I particularly wanted to milk through the summer. One after the other they were all affected, though never with painful swollen quarters, just a few small clots in the foremilk. Normal treatment would clear things up only for the clots to reappear later. We put them all on a five-day course of injections of a different antibiotic, and this seems to have cured the trouble. The final cost of drugs and discarded milk was £150, which underlines how vigilant we must be with mastitis and its prevention.

It would seem to me that there was a tolerance building up to the drugs we were using. A veterinary friend made a most interesting observation about this. He suggested that whilst dry cow therapy was very admirable, the practice of using antibiotics as a routine may have its long-term problems.

In conclusion, may I thank those of you who voted for me [to contribute to *Cowmen Comment*] and say how much I look forward to contributing in the future. I know that I shall have to be very much "on the ball" and I have already resolved to stop checking the daily milk yield on the old gallon chart – though I haven't resolved to throw it away yet!

June 1977

My wife takes visitors in the summer months and, after unpacking, one of the first calls is always the milking parlour. A considerable number are surprised that we have to milk every day, let alone twice.

I have become quite experienced at explaining the "facts of life" to the younger visitors. There are many pointed questions on this subject, usually prompted by a bantam cockerel or a visiting tom cat.

Last Sunday morning, having milked, washed up and done all the other chores before breakfast, I took three young visitors to feed the heifers and sheep which are away on the grass-keep. This took a leisurely hour, and afterwards they suggested that I must be very bored only doing one hour's work a day, and had I ever considered taking a part-time job?

July 1977

Some people complain of difficulty in fetching the cows for milking, but I have a well-controlled dog that usually has the cows home by the time I've made a cup of tea and prepared the parlour.

October 1977

The greatest activity around here lately has been around the yards of the agricultural engineers as everyone rushed to fit safety cabs and frames before the deadline. We fitted our own without much difficulty after we had modified the toolbox with a sledge hammer.

I have heard a lot of farmers complaining about unnecessary trouble and expense, but I can't help remembering about 12 years ago when there was an accident in the woods that adjoin our fields.

The wood itself was not steep, but the tractor in question had got one front wheel off the edge of the stone roadway onto a bank about 4'–5' high. The rear tyres were bald, and so the driver could not back onto the road. He tried to drive forward, locking the front wheels round as he did so. The tractor flopped over, and he was killed almost immediately. I had to pull him out: he was only 15, and I have always thought what a terrible waste of a young life for want of some simple protection.

November 1977

I used to be a regular user of the MMB cell count service, and for the two or three years I used it my rolling average was 200–300,000/ml.

Being fairly satisfied with this, I let the job lapse, and so when we started to get 'free' results recently I was a bit perturbed to find my rolling average around 500,000.

Since then, the readings have all been around 300,000 but the problem is what you do if you're already doing everything you should be.

We use water jets for washing, paper towels for drying, dry cow therapy, teat dipping and machine testing, and I think for much more improvement we would have to adopt a much more rigorous culling attitude.

Whatever we do or think about improving cell counts, one thing seems to be certain – that in the not too distant future, cell count will be taken into account financially, and, with a background of milk surpluses in Europe, our masters in Brussels may use this to put further pressure on milk producers … and probably sooner rather than later.

December 1977

I was very pleased with the analysis of this year's silage, which arrived recently. This is the first year that I have silted all the crop, and the results certainly justify the extra work.

It also proved that it is not necessary to employ sophisticated and expensive machinery to achieve reasonable results. I feel that those of us on smaller acreages should not worry too much about keeping up with modern machinery trends, providing we stick to the simple well-proven rules of silage making. My equipment – consisting of drum mower, single in-line flail harvester and push-off buckrake – has produced a product with a drymatter of 38% and an ME of 10.5.

Having told you of the good things that happen here, it is only reasonable to mention the things that go wrong. First, I had planned a gradual change-over to the silage, taking something like a week to 10 days. The heavy rain in the last four days of October soon put a stop to this, and the cows had to come in to a full winter diet. My mistake was not to cut the concentrate feeding as soon as the cows came in onto the higher maintenance diet, with the result that many of them are scouring and the milk has dropped.

After five days on the silage, the milk has just started to climb again, but I find for the second month running I have to report a drop in yield because of changing a diet too suddenly.

January 1978

Recently I was chatting with some non-farming friends, and they invited me shooting on Boxing Day. I said I might have difficulty getting time off, to which they replied "But it's a Bank Holiday." I had to spell out to them the fact that – as I would be without help over Christmas – I would be working all day. They were amazed. Further conversation revealed that they were having a 10-day break – not that this would have any affect on the other four or five weeks' holiday they had during the rest of the year.

So, when you're milking on Christmas Day, perhaps feeling a little noble that you are working when most of the community are on holiday, don't kid yourself that you're getting a silent vote of thanks, because the majority don't even realise that you're working.

All of a sudden we read in the farming press that super silage is out. After what seems like a lifetime's exhortations from advisers to make better and better silage, I now read that perhaps we've gone a bit too far. Perhaps the machines recommended have become too expensive; perhaps too many light cuts are producing too light a crop.

It's amazing how agriculture goes around in these cycles.

The secret is to farm exactly the same year after year. For five years you will be a pioneer, for five years you will be farming the same as everyone else, and for five years you will be hopelessly out of date. Don't let this worry you, because it will soon be your turn to be a pioneer again.

I've just noticed a similar example in oil marketing.

Twenty years ago no self respecting Young Farmers film show was complete without the story of "Farmer Efficient" who used just one oil for all his different engines and hydraulics. Of course, his neighbour, 'Farmer Inefficient' had a shedfull of half empty drums of about 20 different sorts. Then about 10 years ago, each new tractor that arrived on the farm suddenly had to have this high detergent engine oil or that special hydraulic oil, and, before we know where we were, we were back to the shed full of oil drums. Now – surprise, surprise – you can get one oil that will do away with all this clutter and complication.

February 1978

The prospect of a new year does not fill me with anything but a sense of foreboding as far as dairy farming is concerned. Against a background of massive overproduction in the EEC, if ever our politicians wanted to turn the screws, now is surely as good a time as any.

They have a wide choice open to them: more stringent hygiene checks, payment on cell count, widening the scope of the antibiotic tests, penalties for high sediment content. The list seems endless, and that does not include any straight financial penalties. Meanwhile, we as dairy farmers seem to be rushing, "lemming like", into a sea of overproduction.

I'm afraid I'm as guilty as anyone. I've just ordered a new milk tank. Ours is full now, and, although I had originally intended buying a small secondhand tank to put next to ours, the cost of moving both tanks narrowed the gap considerably, and so I have opted for a new one. Our tanker driver tells me that he is picking up as much milk now as he was in the spring flush last year.

Everyone seems to blame the "peasants" of Europe who

only keep a few cows for the surpluses. I just hope that those of us on the smaller dairy farms in this country won't be "peasants" of 10 years' time.

March 1978

The stricter controls of animal medicines are something I have anticipated for some time. The veterinary profession has seen the scope of its activities eroded for many years now. This has meant an upward spiral of costs as farmers have become more proficient at many of the tasks that would have been the province of a vet 10 years ago.

Where they dragged their feet as a profession was in their attitude to the sale of the multitude of drenches and equipment that are now supplied by the numerous animal health firms that have sprung up over the last decade.

If the vets had secured a larger share of this multi-million pound market, I suspect that we would not be faced with this legislation now.

Professional ethics are all very fine, but the rule that says you must not display the goods you sell in a window next to your surgery is taking things a bit too far. As an industry, we would probably have benefited by having professional advice when we bought their goods.

April 1978

The society we live in is very conscious of its environment. Conservation and the preservation of the balance of nature is the order of the day. As custodians of the land, every activity of our industry is subject to the closest scrutiny. Mindful of our position as a minority, it is imperative that we adopt a responsible attitude to the conservationists, and, if possible, anticipate their demands.

I mention this because there have been several reports recently in the national press regarding the increasing levels of nitrates in water supplies. In some areas the position has become so bad that they may have to 'dilute' supplies with water from other areas. Looming on the horizon are the inevitable EEC regulations, with even stricter controls.

The blame for this situation is put squarely on agriculture's shoulders, and, as dairy farmers, we must surely be near the top of the nitrogen users table. That the situation is serious, there is no doubt, but as an industry, we seem to be adopting an "ostrich-like" attitude. If ever some controls were introduced, the repercussions could be devastating. Better we put our own house in order than have it put in order for us.

Whilst on this subject, it always seems to me that we could do a better public relations job on our own behalf. The farms that make the headlines are usually the ones with several hundred cows or several thousand pigs or hens.

That these farms are a tiny minority is largely ignored by the media, who seem dedicated to informing the public that most of us are engaged in large-scale farming activities which either desecrate the landscape or involve some cruelty to the animals we keep. It would seem that the average farmer spends his week something like this:

Monday:	Bulldoze out hedges.
Tuesday:	Burn fields of straw.
Wednesday:	Empty slurry pit and/or silage effluent into river.
Thursday:	Dip sheep in dip containing hoarded dieldrin.
Friday:	Remove stiles and all other traces of public footpath.
Saturday:	Leave muck on roads in order to mess up cars of weekend trippers.

July 1978

My mastitis control programme continues. We have found over 30 cases in the three months since we started.

At first sight, this seems an alarming proportion, but analysis of the records shows that 10 of these cases occurred in two cows, and, of the remainder, clots were only visible on one occasion and would almost certainly have escaped detection before we started the clear-up programme.

We have now gone two weeks without a fresh case (that's surely tempting providence), and I now look forward to seeing some improvement in my cell count. I shall compare each month's results with last year's, and hope to see some improvement each month.

As for the two problem cows, I have already culled one and have separated the other from the main herd and put her with the "walking wounded" and dry cows, so she is always milked last. She is due to calve in August, and I still hope to have another heifer calf out of her.

The trouble with these cows that are a constant problem is that they may well be adding 100,000 to the cell count each.

October 1978

For some time now I have been concerned that – as an industry in general, and as Friesian breeders in particular – we are devoting too much time and energy to our search for a "super bull". It seems to me that there is far too much money spent, and made, in the top ranks of the pedigree world. As the prices for the top bulls and females soar, ova transplants become the order of the day, and there is a very real danger that sound breeding practice will take second place to the profit motive.

As far as my own breeding policy is concerned, I have changed from my new-bull-every-year system, and, for two years running, have used the bull Rhosithel Nordema, and I have enough semen in store to last me for another two years.

This may seem an 'all your eggs in one basket' policy, but I am satisfied that this bull provides the type of cattle I require, and his long-term use will stamp some type on the herd as a whole, making the choice of the bull that follows easier.

So, not for me the annual search through the glossy semen catalogues: I seem to have put my money on a stayer rather than try to pick a Derby winner every year.

November 1978

My 4/8 abreast is now 14 years old, and I am becoming increasingly conscious that it will soon need some attention.

We are up to 80 cows now, and, when we have finished calving this autumn, there is a danger that the job will become too long and tedious, with the inevitable fall-off in efficiency and care.

On the other hand, I am still convinced that the abreast parlour has some tremendous advantages, and will have a part to play for many years. I shudder to think what would happen to some of my slower milking, high yielders in a herringbone. I am equally aware that there are plenty of herds with herringbones achieving higher yields than I am.

This winter I am going to spend some time investigating the possibility of doubling up my units and installing automatic cluster removal or even extending the parlour into the dairy and making it a 6/12 or 12/12.

February 1979

I make no apology for returning once again to a theme that I have often used before, namely that there is nothing new in farming.

I have never got very excited about tractors. The only difference between most of them, give or take an odd point or two, is the colour. The only exception I have ever heard about is the Ford 7000, which, if the experiences of a lad in our village with a female hiker are anything to go by, are the tractors to have if you want to pull the birds!

However, to return to my "nothing new" theme. One salesman insisted I visit his yard to see the Renault range of tractors. In particular, he mentioned a new feature which allowed excellent access to the engine for routine servicing.

He undid a couple of latches and the whole bonnet pivoted forward. Yes, you've got it, just like a Ferguson TE20.

March 1979

I have been taken aback by the cost of new milking equipment. Even to double up my existing parlour and fit ACR will cost around £6,000 before grant. This seems a lot of money for a fairly marginal increase in output. From my calculations on work routine time, it would only mean an extra six or seven cows an hour. Not a very encouraging return on capital.

This makes me inclined to bury my prejudice and consider a new 10/10 herringbone. A completely new building would only cost around £500 more than altering my present set-up. I was very surprised to find that my local builder could build me a completely new parlour, including loft, for a lot less money than a customer-built prefabricated parlour. I thought his quotation very reasonable: it's the £9–10,000 for stalls and equipment that is giving me second thoughts. The final decision will probably be the bank manager's.

May 1979

I have now completed 12 months with the MMB Mastitis Control Service. Throughout this period, cell counts have remained fairly constantly between 400,000 and 450,000.

In view of these results, it would appear that the exercise has been a waste of time and money. However, on reflection, I feel it has imposed a certain amount of discipline on us. We seem to have reached the stage where cell count improvements will lie in selective culling. I am hoping to increase the numbers of heifers reared, and this will in the long term mean a younger herd and make culling less of a dilemma than I find it at the moment.

After months of deliberation I have finally ordered a new parlour. My preference for the abreast has won through, and I have chosen a Hosier circular abreast. This parlour is the brainchild of Ian Winter, whose Morven Holstein herd gave its name to the parlour.

Basically, it is a 14-stall abreast wrapped around into almost a circle. The segment that is missing is where the cows enter. It requires a building 33' square, which makes for very light and spacious conditions. It is possible to see all the cows from any point, and the circular working area is only 12' across. As I have said before, I was determined to find a parlour which I would enjoy using in 15 years' time, which is the age of my present set-up.

The prospect of working in some of the herringbones I have seen attracted me about as much as working on a production line at British Leyland. I am not necessarily advocating this type of parlour for everyone, merely expressing a personal preference.

I have ordered a 7/14 with ACR, which gives me the option to double up in the future if necessary. It is possible to have 10, 12 or 14 stalls.

I anticipate a throughput of around 50–60 cows an hour, which I find very acceptable, given the individual attention I will still be able to provide. With a 14/14 set-up, outputs of around 100 cows an hour are claimed.

July 1979

I have finally resolved the problem of my high cell count cow. She came bulling last week, which – for a cow due to calve in September and with a 2 million cell count – was a total mistake.

September 1979

The builders have promised to start work on the new parlour today. I had not realised what a protracted business it would be, just to organise all the many facets that are involved.

One of the greatest time-wasters has been obtaining a second estimate for the building work. I had an estimate from my local builder fairly quickly, but no-one else showed any interest at all. I visited a couple of stands at the West Midland show last May and asked for someone to call to quote for the parlour and also a cattle shed I am planning. So far, there has been no further contact – four months later.

I hope that by the next time I write I can report some progress, but, after my experiences so far, I am thinking of the new parlour as a sort of Christmas present.

December 1979

There is no editorial interference in the content of these short articles. We are left to write about anything which we feel is relevant and hopefully of interest. However, the Editor is a stickler for accuracy, and he has insisted that I point out that when I stated in last month's article that I was looking on the new parlour as a sort of Christmas present, I did not say which Christmas I was referring to.

One of the main problems we have experienced this year is abortion. Not, I hasten to add, brucellosis. We have had five cases since the summer, and each has brought its share of worry while we have waited for the results of the tests.

When we became accredited several years ago, we had 12 reactors on the first test. Ministry advice was to use a programme of 45/20 injections and wait until the scheme became compulsory. I was more concerned with the health of my family and the long-term effects on my children's lives if ever they should contract the disease. Accordingly, I sent the reactors for slaughter immediately, and confounded the experts (and myself) by never having a reactor again. A close friend, who is a Ministry vet, was convinced that I would have trouble eventually, and so these recent cases have been a source of worry in case his warning should prove correct.

My own vet is attempting to establish some common factor in the affected animals by means of blood tests.

I've been nagging my builder to get on with the small extension we are having to the cubicle shed. He has blamed his asbestos suppliers up to now, so, when their lorry turned up yesterday, I was hopeful of an early start. My hopes were very short-lived, because the bed of the lorry – which I suspect was overloaded – broke completely in half and deposited in a heap on the yard a load of what will probably prove the most expensive hardcore for miles around.

However, I am confident that our builder will stay here until he's finished all the outstanding work. He has to; we've got all his tools!

The Eighties

March 1980

I heard Sir Michael Edwardes of BL speaking at the beginning of the year about imports and their effect on the economy and employment. He was speaking at a time when steel strikes were just about to begin.

Meanwhile, we as farmers should give the matter a lot of thought. We cannot expect the people who consume our products to continue to do so at a time when we are possibly buying less and less of theirs. If we continue as an industry, to buy imported equipment and eventually contribute to unemployment, then who can blame the unemployed if they buy cheaper foreign imported food?

Installation of the parlour has finally begun, and the stallwork should be completed by the end of this week.

I've just re-read these notes and have wondered if I should set an example regarding my first topic, and ask the bank manager if I can have a new Jag. On reflection, though, I suppose the ultimate status symbol these days must be a bulk cake lorry arriving on the yard.

September 1980

At the time I write these notes we have been using the new parlour for a week.

During recent months, as I have been paying the final accounts for the parlour, I have watched my overdraft increase at an alarming rate. I confess to mixed feelings about whether I made the right decision to proceed. Using the parlour has helped to dispel some of my doubts. The overall improvements in performance and working conditions have made me realise that the expenditure was not premature but overdue.

At a time when margins in dairying are under severe pressure, especially where borrowed money is involved, it represents a long-term commitment to milking. I can well understand the many dairy farmers, who, we are led to believe, are queuing up to go out of milk. Any one faced with capital expenditure must see the EEC handshake as an attractive alternative.

There can be few more disappointing sights in farming, though, than the shambles created in a new parlour during the first milking. When we opened the door for the first time, everything was gleaming and spotless. An hour and a half later there were several barrowfuls of the usual, liberally spread about the walls, stalls and floor.

We've got 75 cows in milk and take about 1¼ hours in the morning. In the old parlour both milkings would have been over two hours.

November 1980

I expect most of us receive notification of an impending TT, or brucellosis, test with an inward groan, and the complacent thought that it will be a waste of time. These were my reactions three or four weeks ago when I was informed one Saturday morning that we would be TT testing the following Monday.

My complacency was completely shattered half way through the Thursday morning when my vet found a reactor. Five minutes later he found another. The reactions were such that a re-test was not considered necessary, and the two cows were eventually sent for slaughter.

The position at the moment is that no trace of TB was found at the post-mortem, although the final all-clear will not come until selected glands have undergone tests in Ministry labs. Obviously, the detection and eradication of TB are the paramount criteria in this, but I still feel a sense of dissatisfaction in the whole business.

We have already tested all cattle not included in the first test, and these were completely clear. But we have to go through another test after the prescribed 60 days. Until then, all cattle movements are out of the question.

We are already starting to accumulate a collection of beef calves we could well do without – confident that they will be worth no more money in 60 days' time than they are now, even though we will have spent time and money feeding them.

March 1981

If, like me, you have always regarded the trades allied to agriculture as having a common interest (that is, what was good for one was usually good for the other), you may also, like me, have had this apparent myth brought into perspective by the man reporting on the grain trade on the early morning farming news, a couple of weeks ago. In reporting a slow trade in most sectors, he stated that both compounders and grain traders were earnestly hoping for a prolonged spell of very hard weather.

I can well understand them wanting this to happen, but I was very surprised that it should be stated so categorically on a programme presumably aimed at the customer who was most likely to suffer from such conditions.

As our interests are apparently not common – and indeed diametrically opposed – it is perhaps just as well that I have already changed my dairy costings from the scheme run by my compounder to the Farm Management Services run by the MMB. One of the first points made by the new adviser was that I was paying more for a ton of cake than I was receiving for a ton of milk.

May 1981

We have just completed our latest TB test – four months after the last – and achieved another all-clear, which makes me hopeful that the problem is resolved once and for all. However, we have to have another test in 12 months' time before we return to normal three-year testing.

Ironically, it was while testing that we came across our first-ever case of hypomagnesaemia.

I have always spread magnesium lime on our grassland, and have used the annual silage analysis to monitor magnesium levels. As they have always been way above average and we have not taken any routine preventative precautions, this has meant a considerable saving in the past, since we have not had to spend money on expensive concentrates such as a vehicle for a daily magnesium intake.

The cow that attracted our attention was shaking violently whilst waiting to be tested and was absolutely panic-stricken when in the crush. A quick drive to the vet's and a bottle under the skin soon put matters right, but two days later my ignorance of hypomagnesaemia was to prove expensive.

When I fetched the cows off the rye for morning milking, one cow was down and clearly close to death. It was obvious that it was too late for any subcutaneous injection, so I rushed back for two bottles of magnesium and proceeded to put one in her vein and one under her skin.

A subsequent discussion with my vet revealed that it was almost certainly the intravenous magnesium that killed her. Apparently, I should have used calcium into the vein and magnesium under the skin. The magnesium content to the calcium bottle would have been enough to keep her going. As the vet remarked, "We used to use intravenous magnesium to put down horses during the war." (He didn't say which war.)

Since then, we have had two cows go berserk in the parlour and have had to take appropriate action. I have made sure that the latest cake delivery had added magnesium, and we are offering a mollassed magnesium mineral ad lib in the feed troughs. The strangest factor has been that all the cows affected so far have been high yielders receiving up to 20lb of cake a day, which I would have thought would have been adequately mineralised.

These days, when it is imperative to keep costs down, any item of expenditure needs to be considered carefully, and all the alternatives looked at. A friend of mine came up with an original money-saver which I found amusing.

He was proposing to put a fore-end loader on a tractor without power-steering, and asked me how much I thought power-steering equipment would cost. I said £400–£500, which he considered out of the question. He now reckons he's got to send away for a body-building course instead!

September 1981

I never thought I would ever see the day, but, I regret to admit, two weeks ago we actually missed a milking. As usual, when something breaks down, the trouble occurred on a Sunday.

I had been off for the day visiting my parents and my heart sank when I returned home at 8.30 pm and saw the cows still about and the local electricity board van in the yard. Apparently the electric motor driving the vacuum pump had burnt out when they had tried to start it.

When something goes wrong at milking time, time itself goes very quickly and when I arrived home they were just trying to wire up an electric motor borrowed from a neighbour. Unfortunately the starter gear and the motor were incompatible and despite all efforts we failed to get started. It was now 10.30 pm, so I phoned the firm who fitted the parlour and arranged for them to bring a new motor out next morning and with great reluctance let the cows go.

By the time the new motor was fitted and minor difficulties such as different shaft sizes overcome it was 10 am. We were down about 100 gallons on that day's milk and it took about five days to get back up to previous production levels. The only bright spot – if that were possible – was the fact that the motor was still three weeks inside guarantee.

If that wasn't enough trauma for the time being, the new motor lasted exactly 11 days before it too burnt out during evening milking. This one managed to blow the fuse on the mains supply into the bargain, and it wasn't until we had tried to milk using the generator, without success, and called out the electrician to check it, that we correctly diagnosed the problem and phoned our Hosier agent. He had us operating on a new motor by 10 pm.

One of our silage fields is next door to the pub (only by coincidence!) and one Saturday, when I was moving some second-cut silage, I was fascinated to watch the meet of the local "mink" hounds. I use the inverted commas because the aforementioned "mink" hounds are in fact redundant otter hounds. As we are all aware, mink are voracious and deadly hunters and will soon clear all the wild life from around pond and river, so the attentions of the mink hunting fraternity are highly commendable. The only factor that has yet to be explained to my satisfaction, is what happens when the "mink" hounds come across your friendly neighbourhood otter?

January 1982

Last month I lost one of the best helpers I have ever had. I am referring to the dog which I had had for about 12 years, which had, without fail, fetched the cows home for milking.

How anyone manages without a good dog I just cannot imagine. They are especially valuable on dark autumn mornings or in the spring when the cows are full of grass and consider the walk home something of a favour.

The secret is, of course, to have some control. You don't want a dog that will bring freshly-calved cows home at 50 mph, widening the gateways in the process. This particular dog always slept outside the kitchen door. One word when I got up in the morning would send her on her way. By the time I had made a cup of tea, prepared the milking equipment and wet the parlour down, she would have the herd well on its way home, despite having to go round 40 acres in four fields of set stocking. I reckon she saved half an hour a milking; something some of us spend a lot of money on milking facilities to do. Her replacement will be difficult.

February 1982

I am loath to complain about the weather because I am well aware from telephone conversations with friends in other parts of the country and from reports in the media that we are much better off than many. Today, three days after the blizzard, we are managing to cope with the day-to-day tending of livestock.

I was particularly annoyed the day after the blizzard by the amount of non-essential traffic about, when priority should have been given to road clearance and stock feeding. I felt very sorry for the MMB tanker driver who collects Channel Island milk locally who battled through to collect milk from a neighbour, and then had to wait over two hours while two articulated lorries loaded with new cars were pulled along the single track road by three four-wheel drive tractors. Surely this sort of traffic should be banned in such conditions?

Finally, on the brighter side, we were surprised to find a

newborn lamb running about in the snow when we went to feed the sheep on Christmas Day. It was out of a ewe I bought in the autumn, and she must have been in lamb then.

If that wasn't surprise enough, when we battled our way to take some hay to the ewes two more ewes had lambed – a set of twins and a single. We took the twins home but we couldn't catch the single, and he has survived without ill-effect. He follows his mother about in the knee-deep snow, appearing at intervals rather like a dolphin.

August 1982

If you want your ego deflating, then walk around the Royal Show all day without anyone trying to sell you some wine. This was my experience, and I am seriously considering buying a new jacket for next year.

September 1982

The big news here at the moment is that for a month we have been milking three times a day. I have been toying with the idea for a long time now. My main concern was regarding the quality of life that this would leave us. It seemed imperative that there should be a third person, employed elsewhere, to help out with some of the night milking. To give the system a fair trial, we decided to try it during the summer holidays so my son could become one of the team before he returned to his school work.

So far it has been an unqualified success. We have consistently been 200–300 litres over target every day. Today's target was 1,450 litres, and we actually achieved 1,730. I have contacted a former employee who now works outside agriculture and he has agreed to do three nights a week.

Anyone contemplating milking three times a day should not underestimate how tiring it can be, particularly when you are busy with silage or baling and carting straw. The biggest social stumbling block so far is Saturday night. Unfortunately, my assistants are all single, and seem to think that I have no business being out on Saturday nights at my age.

October 1982

Our new parlour has been a burden from a financial point of view over the last two years, but is now earning its keep. We certainly would not have contemplated 3x milking in the old parlour. August figures are about 20% up on prediction, and even allowing for the extra costs of electricity and labour we should be about 15% better off.

One of the biggest chores is fetching the cows in the dark evenings. Although we are never short of dogs here, we only have one that I would consider taking to fetch the cows (the others would bring them home at about 50 mph, and we would need new gate posts everywhere). She is a young bitch I am training to work the cows with an eye to the future, but she has just discovered some rabbits in a wood and disappears into the darkness at high speed, leaving me to stir the cows up on my own.

I was amused by the story told by my young assistant, who was fetching the cows in one morning at 5.30 am. They happened to be lying in a field next to two cottages used by city dwellers at weekends. He was calling the cows as normal and was very surprised when one of the occupants came out and cursed him for making a noise: "Didn't he know there were people in bed?" He replied that they were "____ lucky" and proceeded to dazzle the complainant with our new chargeable torch.

It is ironic that these people go to great expense to acquire an occasional rural lifestyle ... providing the sights, sounds and smells are completely to their liking.

The increased output of milk nationally against a background of declining consumption is worrying for all of us. One factor which always concerns me is the actual palatability of the pinta on the doorstep.

We provide farm holidays here, and during the summer there is a large cross-section of the milk consuming public staying here. For many, it is their first contact with farm milk, and they are usually amazed at the difference. They think it's creamier and tastier, and their children drink it with relish. "He never drinks milk at home" is a common comment.

Perhaps we should look to improving the product and the sales would look after themselves.

February 1983

If you read an ADAS bulletin on 3x milking, one disadvantage that is invariable quoted is the possible danger of overfeeding concentrates. We are all aware of the equation of a pound of cake per cow per milking, multiplied by the days in the month, giving as its answer bought milk and reduced margins. Mistakes of this sort are obviously a lot worse if the cows are milked 90 times a month instead of 60!

This was the picture that emerged from our November figures, with the result that our margins were exactly the same as those for the previous November, despite selling a lot more milk. This was a very sobering statistic after a month of late nights and early mornings. Happily, December's results were excellent, but it will be a useful lesson and make me a lot more careful in future. If there is a plus factor involved, it must be that my impression that the cows were in very good condition was confirmed by my freeze brander, and also my butterfats have been better than for some time.

It is common practice to substitute initials in the farming press to avoid frequent repetition of familiar phrases. Some of the more common ones are TBC, snf, bf, MOC. I regret that I shall have to introduce one of my own invention. It is ACHASILW. In full it represents "another cow has aborted since I last wrote". The Ministry vets investigating the problem have drawn a blank, and there is a nutrition specialist calling this morning to see if the answer lies in this area.

March 1983

The day after I wrote my last notes, we had a visit from the regional ADAS nutritionist, accompanied by the Ministry vet who has been investigating our abortion problem. She went through our feeding practices from A–Z and took samples of all the feeds currently in use and these were subjected to exhaustive lab tests.

Her subsequent report could find no fault with our winter feeding programme, which was a bit of a pat on the back, but shed no light on the purpose of her visit. Lab tests on the fodder and concentrate samples revealed nothing, so we are still at square one. As the vet said, "All we can hope for, is that it will go away of its own accord." This is very true but not very satisfactory. Even now the problem still continues.

I must admit to worrying about the current over-production in the dairy industry. No-one seems to have an obvious solution: some pundits advocate quotas: others throw up their hands in horror at the idea.

As production continues to rise, the consumer groups seem at last to have got their wish for "cheap" UHT milk from the continent. While the arguments rage, producers like myself milk three times a day to get even more production. We are currently producing about 100 gallons a day more than we were 12 months ago.

My worry is that eventually someone will have to wield the big stick and reverse the trend. If this happens, I feel that smaller intensive producers like myself, with less alternative options, will feel the cold wind more than most. The only consolation is that any drastic measures to curb production would be politically unacceptable on the continent and in the long term we may well be protected by the vociferous French farmer.

Without wishing to be considered trendy, I must confess to a lot of satisfaction from my modest attempts at conservation. This mostly takes the form of tree planting but it is a job easily neglected and I have handed it over to a friend in the forestry industry. He has planted a lot of trees in odd corners and fenced them in for a very modest sum.

We lost a lot of trees in the drought a few years ago and subsequently to Dutch Elm Disease. Of our total acreage we own 50 and it is amazing how many trees we have managed to tuck away even on this limited scale. The most annoying aspect has been how often the odd corner that would accommodate a tree is found to be immediately below overhead power lines. We have a small wood of about an acre, half of which was cleared by the electricity board, and we have planted a row of permanent hardwoods along its length and filled the centre with Christmas trees. When we start to crop these in two years' time our tree planting and fencing activities should be self-financing.

June 1983

There seem to be a lot of letters about milk quotas in the farming press. The smaller producers are pointing the finger at the larger and accusing them of pushing up production just in case a quota system is imminent. The larger producers think that there would be no problem if it wasn't for a lot of small producers on the Continent. I can see both sides of the argument, though this can sometimes be a disadvantage because you end up sitting on the fence.

The reality is usually somewhere near the middle, though I was interested in a comment from my milk tanker driver the other day. He says he collects three full loads a day. On the first run he goes to 12 farms, on the second and third, two farms each and he is full.

Finally, having mentioned elections, "sitting on fences" and "middle ground" all in the same article I must assure readers that I will try and revert to my usual non-political style next month, as by then you may well be heartily sick of such phraseology. I would also like to point out that my acquisition this morning of two drums of blue teat dip (just to try) do not necessarily point to any particular leanings.

July 1983

I spent a recent wet evening catching up with reading the vast quantities of free farming literature. There were still rumbling repercussions about the *World in Action* TV programme about farming.

I wrote a few months ago about farmers being "set up" by the media. In this programme, the professionals – ie, the NFU – were also set up. In retrospect, I wonder if the widespread indignation by the agricultural industry is not something of an over-reaction. After all, it was only one programme.

On the evening in question, I watched an episode of *Emmerdale Farm*. We are very fortunate in the format of ITV's farming soap opera. Twice a week, at peak viewing time, this fairly realistic programme is concerned with a family livestock farm.

There are hundreds of Emmerdale Farms around the country. They may have different accents, but the situation is basically the same. They have their crises, their cashflow problems, mastitis, ewes dying and sheep rustled. They never burn stubble, fell trees or bull-doze hedges, and at the slightest excuse they leg off to try one "at Woolpack".

Week in, week out they surely portray a worthwhile image to the town-dwelling viewer. The viewer is also left in no doubts as to the 'baddies' in agriculture. These are represented by the infamous 'NY Estates'. These are the big-money farmers who have less regard for conservation and are more concerned with efficiency and productivity, and they are nowhere near as nice as the *Emmerdale Farm* folk.

I sometimes think we are hypersensitive about our own image. As long as this particular programme continues, our image is in very good hands.

October 1983

I heard the story the other day of a farmer who had an old grey mare which had been retired out to grass. She occupied a field which was really a small hill, at the top of which stood a stunted oak tree. Every year the farmer refused to cut his hay until the horse had stood for three consecutive days under this tree. While all his neighbours struggled to make hay in indifferent weather, he waited completely unperturbed until the three days had arrived and then he cut all his fields, and, to the annoyance of all around, usually had excellent results. This continued success, which was accompanied by much boasting, proved too much for some of the younger element in the village, and during a fine spell early in the summer some of them put a halter on the mare and tied her to the oak tree.

After three days, out came the mower: all the fields were

cut down – and it rained nearly every day for a month. (For those of you who may be concerned, I am sure somebody took the mare a bucket of water every night!)

December 1983

As I begin these notes, financial considerations dominate my thoughts. We have just completed our costings for October and achieved similar results to 12 months ago. Obviously, to be better off, this is not good enough.

October's milk price is fractionally less than last year's but the big difference is in concentrate costs. Last year the average cost of all the concentrates we fed was around £138. This year – with cake at £165 and maize gluten at £149.50, lucerne nuts at £124 and some protein pellets at over £200 – we ended up with an average concentrate cost of nearly £160. In the circumstances, we did well to achieve similar results to last year's.

Just for interest, we applied last year's costs to this year's performance and found we would have been £10 a cow better off. A bonus of £870 could mean the difference between a nasty letter from the bank manager and a month's solvency.

I've come to the conclusion that to end up with a million pounds from farming you need £2 million to start with.

I have learned from bitter experience that to write about anything going well in *Dairy Farmer* is a sure prelude to disaster. It may be the weather, crops or animal health: whatever it is, the opposite will soon be true. It seems to be some sort of tempting of providence. It is for this reason that I have not mentioned my abortion problems recently.

We have had six months completely trouble-free.

The words of the Ministry vet investigating the problem – that we could only hope that the problem would go away – seemed to have provided the key. Apparently, though, providence couldn't wait any longer, and we have had three abortions in a month.

As usual, there has been no common pattern. One was at eight months, one at seven and one at five. It is very distressing; I can't help wondering where it will all end. The overriding problem is the financial one, steadily eroding already shrinking margins. You can talk about quotas, penalties, CAP reforms and surpluses till you're blue in the face, but when Mother Nature decides to take a hand she can outdo any measures that a politician may dream up.

March 1984

As I write these notes, agriculture – and dairying in particular – sits in a sort of limbo as we await the outcome of the deliberations on surpluses in Europe. I am writing a week earlier than usual as next weekend I will be making my biennial visit to Dublin to see the Wales–Ireland match and I usually seem to have a headache for a week after.

All the signs at the moment are that we are about to be sold out by the Government as a pawn (or sacrificial lamb?) in the political game being played at the moment.

Meanwhile, the quotas v price freeze controversy continues. Only hindsight will resolve which was the correct option.

If someone could find a way for us to milk 10% less cows and make the same total profit, I for one wouldn't mind.

I also read somewhere that a quota on a free market could be worth around £450 a cow. I for one wouldn't mind that either.

May 1984

I expect by now you will all be heartily sick of reading about the recent EEC agriculture package. I had even considered presenting a set of notes making no mention of the dairy sector proposals, but I'm afraid it's a job to thing of anything else. As I write, details are still filtering through. Nevertheless I will describe my own immediate reactions.

First, to achieve our reduction in output we have gone back to twice daily milking. I envisage milking 2x at least until the end of July. By then I shall be in a better position to judge our quota for the remainder of the year. As the quota is on a litre basis, we shall strive to increase output by increasing the value of the litres we actually sell.

This means that we will try to achieve our spring targets by selling, for example, 18 litres/cow/day of high-compositions quality milk, rather than 22 litres/cow/day of lower-value milk from fewer cows.

When the milk price rises in summer and early autumn, we will possibly go back to 3x milking to achieve our maximum output at the new higher seasonal price.

We intend to accumulate some first-cut silage in bags so that high yields in late summer won't be jeopardised by a shortage of grazing. Conversely, we may well restrict spring grazing and supplement it with treated straw to restrict milk output/cow and improve compositional quality.

Because of its fairly predictable impact, I see the increasing strategic use of 3x milking as a management tool to achieve quota levels. It is vitally important that as a nation of milk producers we achieve as near as possible the whole of our allowance quota. There are almost certainly further production cuts in the pipeline, and it is important that they are based on what we are allowed this year and not on an artificially low level that may have been affected by, for example, a dry summer or a late spring.

An over-reaction in the use of beef bulls on our dairy cows could have the same effect in years to come. If we do now produce every drop of milk that we are allowed, then there are plenty waiting in the background to make up any shortfall. Most of us will have to rethink our businesses. It is all very well to talk of reducing overheads. But staff come in units of one. And many of us on smaller farms have only one assistant. Bank interest is a big problem on many farms, but how do you reduce borrowing when profits levels are so low?

Equally, what will we do if we've reached our annual quota with three weeks of the milk year to go? Buy some pigs? Or store the stuff and feed it to Friesian bull calves? Time will tell.

Some things of course, will never change. It's 4 April outside and it's snowing. The grass hasn't grown for over a fortnight. My feed supplier can't get any more beet pulp. The silage is running out fast. And a fox is taking my lambs.

I leave you with this thought: when it comes to Irish jokes is it not a case of "He who laughs last, laughs loudest"?

June 1984

Amidst all the gloom, there is inevitably a lighter side. The agricultural correspondent in our local weekly paper reported last week that there were over 900 "barren" cows in Shrewsbury market. This was followed by much concern about dairy farmers taking panic measures. On the next page, the official market report quoted the actual number of cows as 505. The auctioneer who actually sells these cows is a friend of mine, and he confirmed the 505 as correct.

Another acquaintance had a similar experience in Hereford market. He met one dairy farmer who told him there were 1,000 cows in Gloucester the week before. After much "ooh-ing and aahing" – the mutterings of doom and gloom, – they went on about their business. My friend went round the corner and met another dairy farmer, whose first words were, "There were 2,000 cows in Gloucester last week."

August 1984

Today – 8 July – the quota row rumbles on. I take my hat off to the Dyfed Action Group who have kept the problem in the forefront of national news while the rest of us have done nothing. Their militant action has largely been sympathetically received by the media. Whatever else they have achieved, their most important contribution is to bury once and for all the notion that agricultural opinion is of no significance. The Government has been embarrassed to have a hitherto peaceful section of society taking militant action. The £50 million out goers scheme, imperfect through it may be, must be largely down to them. I am seriously considering sending them my proxy forms for the MMB elections. I do not agree with all their views but their overall aim of perpetuating the viability of the smaller family dairy farm is one with which I readily identify and they deserve all the support they can get.

My delight, a couple of weeks ago, to find burnt-out wiring to the condenser on the milk tank and an agitator paddle that had been stirring warm milk all night, thus creating my own personal butter mountain, was only heightened by the milk cheque that arrived a couple of hours later. The amount deducted for "seasonal adjustment" left me thinking that if I hadn't sold any milk at all, it might have come to more money.

As I bucketed out the sour milk for a friend to feed to his quota pigs the loss didn't seem quite so great. This same friend who is my freeze brander, has now started selling semen for a newly formed company called Black & White Sires. He farms on a County Council holding and faced with a high rent he sees this as one way to make up his quota gap. I only mention this because he said he'd take me out for a meal if I did!

September 1984

The agricultural press is full of fictitious examples of the financial effects of quotas on different farms. I've just been reading one relating to a 500-acre milk and cereal farm. The projected margins for March '85 were £7 an acre or £3,500.

If those figures were to apply to my size of farm, I can foresee a lot of dairy farmers trooping down to the Post Office every Thursday with their Social Security Giro cheques.

One of my own attacks on fixed costs was to ask my only employee to see if he could find another job. Fortunately, he found one locally fairly soon – basically because other people knew what a good reliable employee he was. This didn't make my task any easier. He had lived with us as family since he left school, and it took me about three weeks to summon up enough courage to break the news to him. It wasn't his fault that quotas were imposed any more than it was mine.

If ever Mr Jopling came within range and I happened to have an egg in my pocket I should only be too delighted to dispose of the egg in a suitable fashion. During the few minutes it took him to clean himself up, he would perhaps consider some of the human problems he has created as well as financial.

Like John Trunch I have just received a letter from William Renton, 8 Queen Street, Campbeltown, Argyll. He and some friends are determined to keep, as he puts it, "the stink" going. He is convinced that although things are bad enough at the moment, if we don't continue a campaign against the Government, they could well be a lot worse next year.

He enclosed a car sticker proclaiming 'Thatcher is killing British Dairying' and added that: "I'm not really a car sticker person, but I'm off not to put mine in the back window".

November 1984

I'm thinking of giving up this dairy farming. I'm at the right age for a career change and an opportunity has opened up and I'm seriously considering taking it. I refer, of course, to the opportunity to sit on a "Local Panel Dairy Produce Quota Tribunal".

The opportunities for the future are endless. After we've sorted out the milk quotas, there'll be the grain quotas, then six months in the south of France on the wine quotas, and, who knows, after about 10 years I might make a chairman, and then I would really be on what Arthur Daley would describe as "a nice little earner".

It is obvious that the Government will use quotas and not prices to limit commodities that are in surplus because that way there are so many opportunities for reducing unemployment at the same time.

There is only one nagging doubt at the back of my mind that makes me hesitate before I take the plunge. Would I be able to adjust to the higher standards of living?

I am readjusting to the new situation of less help on the farm. I only have the young school leaver here for three days a week now, and the biggest problem is finding someone to blame if anything goes wrong.

Most the reaction – all hostile – to my "Thatcher's killing British Dairying" car sticker, has come from true-blue beef, sheep and corn farmers. Is their turn to come? I ask myself (half hopefully). I've taken if off the car now and put it on the kitchen wall. We're having a cheese and wine here next week for the church, and its prominent position just being the bar will give me an opportunity to stir them all up again.

February 1985

If there's one aspect of the festive season that annoys me, it's being asked if I had a good Christmas ... or, even worse, a good holiday. These questions are usually directed by someone from the non-farming fraternity who has just enjoyed a 10-day break (which does not necessarily erode into a month's annual leave). Such people find it incomprehensible that I might have been out milking on Christmas evening whilst they were belching in the chair and watching *Indiana Jones and the Temple of Doom*.

Quickly sensing that they might be on thin ice, they move quickly on to ask, not if, but when I am going skiing. As I don't really mind working at Christmas, but would really like to go skiing, the metaphoric ice becomes even thinner.

In fact 12 months ago (in those halcyon pre-quota days) 1985 was to be the year when I actually went skiing. Financial considerations have caused this to be postponed to make it next year I shall have to sacrifice my biennial rugby trip Dublin.

Counter-attack

Meanwhile, back on the farming front the attacks go on.

Last week's *Sunday Times* carried an article about increasing iodine levels in milk. This is apparently due to feeding extra iodine and dusting pastures in deficient areas, and, of course, to teat dipping. It can result in over-active thyroid problems in humans.

Like most things, the problem has to be looked at in perspective, but unfortunately this doesn't sell many newspapers, and the alarmist approach is usually chosen.

An MMB spokesman had apparently quoted the need to drink five pints of milk a day, every day, for problems to occur. If everyone drank milk in these quantities, we could probably afford to cosset our cows' teats with a whole range of expensive, harmless, skin care products.

As I said to start with, another attack, and one to be taken seriously.

April 1985

I've just had the result of my appeal to the quota tribunal. it makes fascinating reading.

The tribunal has decided to award me "a further five cows at an average yield of 6,693 litres, resulting in a secondary quota of nil litres."

The calculation is as follows:

5 x 6,693 = 33,465 litres extra.

First 7.5 % annualised quantity attracts nil quota = 43,672.

Balance = nil.

Balance attracts 100% quota = nil.

Thank you very much.

July 1985

Little but good

With farming going through a difficult political patch, the agricultural press is full of rumblings from the various pressure groups. It seems odd that most of the questions, most of the answers, and indeed most of the original thinking, seem to be coming from the smaller groups.

The Smallfarmers Association, Tenant Farmers Association and the Dyfed Farmers Action Group are collectively accumulating more column inches than the more established NFU. We can only assume that the NFU is quietly beavering away behind the scenes with its much publicised political lobby. I wonder if this is enough. Apparently, they are seeking a 6% subscription increase whilst we are expected to manage on 1.5%. I would like to see a more active and vociferous NFU; one that apparently gave better value for money; one with new ideas for today's new circumstances.

The MMB doesn't come out of today's press unscathed. Seasonal adjustments, low producer prices and the cow vote saga are particular points of discontent.

Meanwhile the Ayatollah of Thames Ditton doesn't appear to care. What is even more worrying is that he knows that he doesn't appear to care, and he doesn't seem to care about that either. His posture bears unfortunate similarities to that of "She Who Must Be Obeyed" in Downing Street. He has even taken to publicly admonishing his own "wets" though apparently in much stronger language.

August 1985

My neighbour has parcels of land dotted about over a 10-mile radius, so we seem to spend a lot of time driving tractors on the road. This provides an excellent opportunity to see what everyone else is doing, which, for someone as nosey as me, is of great interest.

My favourite venue is the harvesting we do on his land high up in the hills adjoining Offa's Dyke. Even in the most humid conditions there is always a fresh breeze to make things more bearable. There are wonderful views in all directions.

The sky is the domain of the buzzard, the curlew and low-flying fighter planes. The land is occupied by suckler cows, sheep and hippies. The latter are few compared with last year, when there was a large commune on some common land just up the road. They were very much a law unto themselves and the road past their camp was a veritable no-go area. Petrol tanks were siphoned, diesel tanks emptied, tractor batteries disappeared, over a wide area. There was always the smell of roast lamb downwind of the camp in the evening.

This year police and local authorities are much more vigilant, and so far there are much smaller numbers about.

It says much for the sartorial elegance of your contributor that a walk down the road to use a telephone to report a puncture should be interrupted by two policemen in a BMW and careful interrogation.

Centre of interest this year lies in the opposite direction: in the large garden of the house adjoining my own hay field. Here, much to the amusement of the younger members of our harvesting team, the occupant has taken to tending his garden completely naked.

It doesn't look particularly comfortable – especially with so many flies about intent on making a meal of anything that moves – but he seems to have got into the swing of it. His one concession is to wear shorts when using a strimmer.

Still, on a hot day with a field full of bales in front of you, it is a diversion, and there is much talk amongst the younger element of investment in catapults.

Milk bar

Of a more serious nature, and yet in some ways just as ludicrous, is the letter I have before me now. It comes from the MAFF and is entitled "The Milk (Special Designation) Regulations 1977 as amended".

Briefly, this relates to my authorisation to sell untreated milk to guests of our farm holiday business.

It relates to a routine visit many years ago, by our dairy husbandry adviser, who noticed our B & B sign and said we needed this dispensation to sell untreated milk to our guests.

Since then our milk has been subject to regular sampling and testing in addition to the normal testing carried out by the dairy. I would add that we have always passed these tests.

The changes recently made to the regulations prohibit all catering sales, including those made by way of farmhouse bed and breakfast accommodation. This takes effect from 31 October.

So that's it. Fair enough, the interests of public health must be paramount. I accept that, but I did seek clarification from my local NFU office.

Now we come to the interesting bit. According to them, the situation is as I stated it, but I could if I so desired, sell untreated milk in a farm shop or on a milk round!

Can you imagine it?

"Cornflakes, Mrs Smith? Certainly, but if you want milk on them you'll just have to pop up the yard and buy a pint in the farm shop."

Alternatively, I could buy a white smock, a blue striped apron and a straw hat and make a circuit of the dining room, rattling a hand crate at the appropriate time.

Naturally, I will not resort to any of these methods. Of course, I shall buy "proper" milk for our guests from the milkman. But I'm ever so worried in case we get it mixed up in the fridge.

Warren peace

I had noticed that rabbits were on the increase around here, but I didn't realise to what extent until I looked over the hedge and surveyed their depredations on my neighbour's winter barley. Accordingly, I set forth one evening in the Land Rover with a shotgun across my knee. With the passenger window open I was able to drive around my grazing fields and in half an hour, shooting out of the open window had accounted for 27.

I nearly made one expensive mistake. The gun was completely inside the cab, one rabbit had started to move and I had started to follow it ... but I just managed to stop in time. It shows how many there are about. I shall leave the rest until they are a bit bigger and sell them in Hereford market. When your only source of pocket money is what you receive from *Dairy Farmer*, any extra income is very welcome.

All change

Just as I was about to pop these notes in the post, my local NFU office phoned. A "concession" has occurred regarding the "milk for guests" saga. You can now serve untreated milk in farmhouses provided the guests are made aware that it is untreated – so, presumably, they can opt for pasteurised milk if they wish.

I wonder if this concession has occurred because the previous situation was unworkable and unenforceable?

September 1985

Drug pedlars

There is much in our local papers and the national farming press about a combined police and pharmaceutical society operation against a network marketing illegal drugs and growth promoters. It is fairly common knowledge in this area that these products are available. There is even a story of a farmer phoning a manufacturer for advice on the use of a spray, only to be told that the spray was banned in this country.

There are two worrying aspects about this. First, we all know that the products are supposed to come from across the water from "you know where". The products themselves are readily available over the counter there, however.

It has been suggested that some of them were originally stolen by "you know who" to raise funds for their activities. That in itself hardly needs supporting.

Second, the non-farming press give the impression that the use of these products is so widespread that every domestic animal and bird is saturated with them. Some of the reports I have read conjure up visions of whole herds of cattle being sprayed with antibiotics by helicopter. The assumption seems to be that anyone who buys antibiotics that have fallen off a lorry will be equally irresponsible in their use. I have a friend whose company makes its living by selling animal health products and he has been hard hit by these illegal activities – and that is only the growth promoters and anthalmintics that are legally available. He is adamant that only the prosecution of farmers and the attendant publicity will halt the trade. I am well aware that the antibiotics that are provided by my vet appear to be expensive but I am quite happy about that. I consider it to be one of the prices I pay for the peace of mind that comes from the knowledge that he runs a 24-hour service.

If you think that your vet charges plenty anyway, just have a look to see what he charges his small animal clients!

If the recent activities of police and others have halted this trade I for one will welcome it. Our industry can well do without the adverse publicity it brings with it.

As you were

NFU headquarters in London phoned this morning (phew). Apparently the final paragraph of my last article was wrong.

The situation regarding the provision of untreated milk for farmhouse guests is as I first described it.

Briefly, untreated milk cannot be provided for farmhouse guests but it can still be sold in a farm shop or sold on a milk round. The amendment that I printed – namely that untreated milk could be served providing the guests were made aware that it was untreated – was a concession sought by the NFU but which the Ministry refused.

October 1985

Double trouble

I rarely venture political opinions, but, like everyone else, have my own views about individual politicians.

Bottom of my personal league in recent years has been John Gummer. He has always struck me as a bit of a clever-clogs and lacking in real substance.

I regard his arrival at the Min of Ag with dismay, and can only compare a Jopling–Gummer double act with the two goats who were put in charge of a cabbage patch.

Events may prove me wrong, but I suspect that between them they will be about as much use to agriculture as an ashtray on a motorbike.

June 1986

The recent events in Chernobyl have brought such a disaster closer to home than any of us have ever dared to contemplate.

I suggest that in future, food production in excess of consumption is prudent; a reserve in store something to be cherished.

Whilst milking on Sunday morning, in torrential rain, the voice on the radio news informed that due to heavy rainfall, radiation levels were much higher than anticipated. It was raining so hard at the time that I half expected the cows to come into the parlour, glowing like children in a Ready Brek advert.

I sometimes wonder if the authorities tell us the whole truth about nuclear power stations and radiation. I for one am quite happy that there are organisations like Greenpeace about to keep an eye on things.

July 1986

Tough luck

My recent milk production has been beset by problems of a more serious nature.

I am a fairly simple person. (Simple being a kinder adjective than thick). I know that if I give my cows fibre, such as hay, it will help to keep my butterfat levels up.

Similarly, if I keep up energy levels, by feeding beet pulp, it will help to keep up protein levels.

So what, therefore, do you do, in the middle of May, when your cows are eating 8 lb of hay and 4 lb of beet pulp each, plus grazing, plus cake in the parlour for spring calvers, and the Board's computer writes to tell you, via the notification service, that your milk (3.3 bf) composition is at unprecedented low levels?

The simple answer, given that our Board is already deducting over 2p a litre under what is laughingly known as its seasonal discount scheme, is nothing.

The whole trouble with the scheme is that it takes no account of the vagaries of the weather.

Out for the count

I had become rather complacent about my TBC results. We had settled into a routine that seemed to keep us in Band A with little difficulty. But about 12 months ago, completely out of the blue, we had a result of 60. The following week's result was back to a normal low level.

I phoned the Board and a very nice lady explained that an odd result like that would be disregarded.

In April we had another 60, which I took little notice of, assuming that the tanker driver had had his thumb in the sample bottle. Consternation a week later. Another 60!

There was much rushing about looking for some milk-stone remover. This was put through the system, thought there was no obvious effect.

We are now back to 01 and 03, and back in our previous routine, but April's Band A bonus is gone for ever.

May 1987

Although we always consider dairy farming our main occupation, the farm holiday side of our business is extremely important and may well, in the future, play an increasingly important role. To the average visitor from an urban background, cows and milking are of limited interest. So I have always made sure that we have a collection of "odds and ends" about the place.

Collecting eggs from free-range hens and feeding lambs on bottles can be a focal point to some children's holiday. That is why we always have one sow (whose piglets run free about the place – until they find their way into the garden), a Jacob ewe, a Dorset Horn ewe, a few ducks, and so on.

Sometimes providing these extra interests can backfire. For example:

Question: "What are those pretty little grey birds called?"

Answer: "Those are guinea fowl."

"Children, come and look at these beautiful guinea fowl."

Next morning: "Those damned guinea fowl were making a hell of a noise at 5 o'clock this morning."

Or: "Can I take the sheepdog up to the caravan to play with the children?"

Two hours later: "Your dog has been up on our table and eaten half a pound of cold ham and a fruit cake!"

Pride of place amongst these odds and ends is now held indisputably by Percy, our newly-acquired peacock. He and his wife are this season's new interest.

(This is my second attempt at peacock farming. Percy Mark I only lived for six weeks, and the loss of the £35 I paid for him still rankles.)

Percy Mark II is a terrible show-off and during his day visits every group of animals on the farm to perform his display. Fortunately, we are well used to poseurs here, receiving as we do frequent visits (usually at meal times) from students at the Welsh Agricultural College.

June 1987

There are MMB elections due in this area in June, and we have three candidates seeking to become the working man's Steve Roberts. As yet, I know nothing about one candidate, one has milk producing and retailing interests and the other has presumably attended more committee meetings than most of us have had milking times.

It is not inappropriate, at such an election time, for dairy farmers to give some consideration to the recently published report on the demise of Welsh Quality Lamb.

However dedicated and well meaning the directors of this ill-fated organisation, it would seem that as a body they were way out of their depth. Yet compared with the massive scale of MMB operations, WQL was very small beer indeed.

I make no apology for returning to a theme I raised a few years ago – namely that many prospective board members have no commercial experience on a scale even remotely approaching that upon which they seek to participate.

At the time of my previous column, I suggested that some of these candidates should place advertisements in the *Financial Times* seeking directorships in companies of similar scale, just to see how many offers they received.

To illustrate my argument I even composed a fictitious advert which I thought described, in broad terms, the type of candidate we were offered. Unfortunately, this completely fictitious effort must have carried more than a ring of truth with it. The very day that that edition of *Dairy Farmer* appeared, I received a phone call from a candidate in an MMB election accusing me of making a personal attack on him.

We now have new elections, with a new crop of candidates. Should we, I wonder, perhaps be looking outside agriculture for some board members?

Why not look for and hire board members with proven expertise, flair and experience from other sectors of the food and drink industry? Why can't I vote for the bloke who sold us all those expensive creameries conveniently before quotas arrived, making a large percentage of their capacity obsolete?

You don't need brains to run a successful organisation as long as you've got enough brains to appoint someone who can do the job.

August 1987

Soured cream

A couple of weeks ago I had the pleasure of meeting rather a well-known producer-retailer. Although 80% of our conversation was about rugby, we did spend a little time on agriculture in general, and milk production and sales in particular.

I was most interested to hear that over 30% of his doorstep sales were of skimmed or semi-skimmed milk. Much of this percentage had accumulated over the last two years.

His problem was that the more skim he sold the more cream he had to dispose of. The price of cream was the same as a couple of years ago, and it was difficult to sell. He even admitted to giving quite a lot to the pigs. (It's a good job I'm not feeding his pigs for him: I'd be 20 score within a fortnight.) With producers still being paid for butterfat, this is ironic. But no doubt his experiences are typical of the dairy industry as a whole. We shall have to think more in terms of milk as a source of protein and calcium in future.

What amazes me is the speed at which consumers have adopted these so-called healthy habits. The evidence against smoking has not had the same effect.

I was talking to someone in the pub the other day, and he was telling me he only drank skimmed milk now. He said this with an air of self-satisfaction – though I think he was on the sixth pint and tenth fag at the time.

September 1987

Caught flatfooted

Crises are part of farming. We all suffer them, and all learn to cope with them in our different ways.

We recently suffered just such a crisis. One of such immense proportions that the whole farm nearly ground to a halt. The men of this family have a very bad habit (so we have been told thousands of times) of kicking off our wellies outside the kitchen door during the summer months, when they are discarded during the daytime for more suitable footwear.

Unfortunately, our dustbins are also placed not far away from the kitchen door as well. Disaster struck when a fastidious refuse collector removed the contents of our bins along with three pairs of D-registration wellies.

December 1987

Dignified exit

I've always had a conscience about disposing of my old cull cows. I've got three cows here at the moment that I bought as fresh-calved heifers in 1973. I remember the date accurately because I thought I'd been ripped off.

These cows are still fit and in calf, but commonsense tells me they ought to go soon. That is why I am delighted that our local knackerman has opened a conventional abattoir specialising in cull cows, and has equipped a lorry especially for dealing with casualty or sick animals.

A fourth cow to the three I mentioned previously had to go a couple of months ago because she couldn't get up the steps in the parlour. She went on a nice clean lorry, on her own, confined enough by divisions to stop her being knocked about on the journey. Up the ramp she went without any prompting (I'd told her she was going to the grass keep for a couple of months) with a pat on the backend as a farewell. A bit of a softie? I don't care.

April 1988

Our TBC average for January was seven. On the morning of Saturday 20 February I was taking a very rushed breakfast. That was after some rushed feeding, rushed milking and rushed scraping (though the scraping wasn't as rushed as it might have been, because, if you try to change gear too quickly on our Dexta, the gear lever comes out of the selectors and you have to take the top off the gearbox and poke about with a screwdriver).

The reason for all this haste was the Wales v Scotland stand ticket which was clutched in my left hand in case I forgot it. No-one seems to understand that although the match doesn't start till 2.30 pm, you've got to be down in Cardiff by 10.55 am. They sometimes open early on matchdays. In between mouthfuls, my spare hand was sorting through the post.

The only envelope that seemed to merit further scrutiny was the MMB results notification envelope. If I needed food for thought for my journey, I certainly found it in a TBC result of 135. As there had not been any changes in our recent hygiene routine, there was no reason to suppose that the problem lay in that area. I suspected that the trouble may lie with a heifer that had had a very nasty skin infection and had to all intents lost two quarters. We immediately withheld her milk from subsequent milkings.

Next week I discovered a flaw in the benefits of the notification service. It had taken a whole week to receive news of the first problem. The next letter told us that we had had another test on the 18th of the month. This was also 135. We had, therefore, accumulated two very bad results before we had had any opportunity to take remedial action.

Would it be possible for bad, results like this to receive some sort of priority – even a phone call – especially when they are completely out of line compared with recent past performance?

May 1988

Heavy day

All this took place during a peaceful milking. About once a fortnight, though, you have the sort of milking when you wish that a machine gun was standard equipment in a milking parlour.

I had such an experience the other day. A diminutive heifer had come back in through the parlour exit. There were soon five or six cows backed up in front of her.

When she thought she had enough to cause the maximum amount of trouble she shunted them all violently backwards until the end one was forced into the corner where I put the broom and the hand scraper. Both handles were quickly broken.

While all this was going on, 11 guineafowl flew in and perched on the cake conveyor. They like me to switch it on so they can ride round and round the parlour.

Amidst all this cacophony, I could hear snatches of a report on the radio farming news about a squabble at MMB headquarters about who should be chief executive.

After I had restored order in the parlour, I was moved to wonder if the Board and their executives wouldn't be better off running a sweet shop, or would that tax their abilities too much?

One bad apple ...

We've just had a traumatic month on the milking side. Last month I mentioned having had two TBC tests of 135. That took us into Band C for February and we suffered a hefty deduction from our milk cheque.

I must admit that, with the benefit of hindsight, I was a bit slow reacting to the situation. We've always been in Band A, so I assumed that our hygiene routine must be somewhere near OK. Likewise, our cell counts have been running at 270-300, so I didn't think we'd have too much trouble there.

As I said once before, I pulled a suspect heifer out of the herd and hoped the problem would go away. It didn't; it got worse.

Next we attached the plant, changing from cold washing to conventional hot water washing, twice a day. Still no improvement. Unfortunately, time keeps racing away. Each time you try something new, you have to wait three days for the milk sample to incubate and give a result.

A useful tool in all this proved to be the digital thermometer I use to check carcase temperatures in my game business. Apart from checking water temperatures, it turned up the useful fact that our tank was switching off at 8°C though the tank thermometer showed 5°C. In desperation I phoned my friendly ADAS County Dairy Husbandry Adviser – something I should probably have done much sooner. He was on the yard that afternoon with a microbiologist, and they took milk samples from batches of seven cows as they came through.

Two days later we discovered that batch 8 had scored 450,000. This has resulted in a tank cell count of 190,000. The offending organism was *Streptococcus Uberis*.

Tests for organisms related to plant hygiene were good, indicating that once the mastitis problem was overcome we should be well within Band A.

The cows within batch 8 were subject to very close foremilk scrutiny, and one quarter on cow 38 had no clots but was obviously of a different consistency. This one quarter out of the 80-odd cows we were milking was the cause of all the trouble. No 38 was immediately banished to the calf suckling department, though an offence of this nature carries an eventual death penalty.

We will have further deductions from our March milk cheque, and the whole business will have been financially very painful. I suppose the real culprit is complacency and short cuts. We don't take foremilk before milking, though I know we should. Perhaps in future we will have to.

July 1988

Witch report

Everybody seems to have heifers with warts these days. I know you're supposed to be able to grind them up and make an injection out of them but we never seem to get around to that. I've got one such heifer now. No 52. If you cut her udder off and put it in an aquarium, it would pass quite nicely for a coral reef.

Anyway, there's this woman comes into the pub. She reckons she's a District Nurse, but we all know her granny was a witch. I've seen her buy warts off people for 2p and after a bit the wart goes.

I had a word with her about No 52, and she gave me £1 for her warts. Believe it or not, I think they're starting to go. I had started pulling them off – one a milking but this new method seems much more agreeable. For her previous successes, it has been customary for the beneficiary to buy her a gin and tonic. I dread to think what it's going to cost me if she succeeds, though I have thought of setting up as her agent.

September 1988

Money can't buy ...

Recently, many columnists in the farming press have spent some time deliberating on the sudden inflation of some farming assets – in particular, barns for conversion, surplus cottages and land for development. Most of them have been concerned about the long-term effect on rural life as as we know it. I heard the story the other day of a friend of a friend (an authentic story, nevertheless) who had farmed away fairly happily for 20-odd years on 100 acres. He's just sold a third of his farm for over a million pounds.

My friend reckons he's a changed man. He's not happy any more; he worries about his tax problems; his farming no longer presents a challenge and an interest. He has too much leisure time; too much money.

At first mention they sound like problems we'd all like to have. But I related it to my own situation. I don't want to live anywhere else. I don't want a better car than I've got now. My overdraft is a burden, but it keeps me on my toes (though it would be very attractive to give my bank manager the Harvey Smith one day). I don't want to start drinking in lounge bars. I want to keep all the good friends, from all walks of life, that I've got now.

So I'm basically a contented person. I know I'm lucky to feel that way. Despite the trials and tribulations of farming, not many of us would seek to do anything else, and most of us live a life that many people aspire to.

February 1989

One bad apple ...

We've had a few bad weeks on the cell counts. Actually, we were in Band B for November, but I wouldn't want anyone to know. Fortunately, we had enough confidence in our plant cleaning routine to look at the cows first, rather than waste time checking pipes and jars like we did last year. We pulled the milk out of two cows immediately, and we've seen an improvement since.

I've sent some individual samples off to ADAS and we could well see some culling soon. I sometimes wonder if it would be possible to incorporate individual cell counts as an optional extra with NMR. I know the recorders have enough to worry about at milking time without having to split all the samples, but it would be well worthwhile if we could build up a picture of a cow's cell counts throughout a lactation. Persistent offenders could be identified and culled.

I know from our traumatic experiences of last year that one "rogue" cow can distort the whole picture.

I've always suspected that standards could be further tightened. Today's Band A could be the Band B of tomorrow. Regular individual cell count information could help to put us on the right road.

Tickling the palate

We always feed our cows a high phosphorous mineral in the winter. We've used the same one for some time now.

We put some on top of the silage and there's always some in an old metal wash trough that also contains some rock salt.

This year the cows' appetite for the mineral can only be described as voracious. I think they'd eat two bags a day if we put it out for them. As I'm fairly sure that they are not suffering from any deficiency, I can only assume that the manufacturer has gone a bit over the top with the spices. At the moment you only have to enter the yard with a bucket and they all run out of the cubicles.

April 1989

Anybody who has ever worked with me will tell you that I never do anything wrong. Especially if I can blame someone else. As for actually admitting a mistake, this must be the first time ever.

We've had a few mastitis problems lately, so about a month ago I set off round the cubicles with a very large bucket of (I must be careful here) powder manufactured to kill the bugs in cubicle beds. No need to read the label, so I gave all the beds a good "doing".

Three days later most of the cows were losing the skin off their teats. After five days it was taking $1\frac{1}{2}$ hours to milk and $1\frac{1}{2}$ hours to put grease on the cows' teats. Some were so sore we had to grease them before we milked them.

Some of the worst cases had mastitis, and I am afraid it was all down to me.

Tell us another one

I've spent the last week trying to get a speaker for our annual rugby club dinner. I'm not one for name dropping, but I wonder if, like me, Phil Bennet, Eddie Butler and Gareth Davies put the phone down, returned to their families at the fireside and announced nonchalantly, "I've just been speaking to Roger Evans"?

July 1989

Fair dinkum

Shearing proved to be particularly enjoyable.

We had an 'Australian' in the team shearing this year. I thought I could pay him with a few beads and trinkets, and give him grubs from under the bark of trees for his lunch, but he wanted paying the same as the others.

He's actually a member of a local family that emigrated 10 years ago, and he rejoices in the traditional Aboriginal name of Lewis Pugh.

Despite this, there was plenty of "too right" and "oh, my word" and "walkabout" punctuating the conversation – all I may add, from the local shearers.

I had to slow them down a bit towards the end because the missus said that if we finished early I'd got to take her out. As it was, we had a good evening out afterwards.

Someone said: "What are you lot celebrating?"

I said: "The end of shearing."

"How long have you been shearing?"

"Just today."

Our "Australian" still hasn't come up with a satisfactory explanation for his wife why he didn't get home till 3.30 am. I think he was supposed to take her out as well.

Country living

The problem of local housing for local people is frequently in my thoughts.

The ripples from the pebble of prosperity, that was tossed into the waters of the South East, are still just reaching this area. The reaction – slowly, but apparently inevitably – is having an appalling effect on our community. Will future historians view it as having the same importance that we accord the agricultural and industrial revolutions of previous centuries? Just four or five years ago, there were plenty of houses available around here for £20,000. Those same houses are now selling for £50–£60K. I read in the paper that a £50K mortgage costs around £500 a month ... but there are plenty of decent local people earning less than £150 a week, so where will they live? No-one seems to be doing anything about it; no-one seems to care.

I was appalled to find a local lad, in full employment, living rough. He's now living in a 12' caravan up in our yard.

The only enquiries I've had about his welfare are: a) has he got planning permission to live there and b) who's going to pay his poll tax? No-one seems worried about finding him something better for the winter.

Most of the "cheaper" housing is going to newly-retired couples who have sold a house elsewhere and can come into this area, into similar accommodation but with the added bonus of some capital in the bank.

There was just such a couple in the pub last week.

Only been in the area a week, and sitting in our seats already. The cosy little corner where we regulars – rural philosophers all – have our daily chat.

We don't talk about fertiliser to put on your second-cut silage like they do in the adverts. We're more interested in who's blown his forage harvester up, whose cheques are bouncing, sex and violence and other rural matters.

Anyway, we squeezed ourselves in around these infiltrators, who were obviously fascinated with our conversation. (I think someone's cow had put its bed out that night.) They gradually joined the discussion.

Londoners. Sold a house for a lot of money. Bought a much

cheaper home and new car (in London). Money in the building society. Thought the local shops were very expensive, so they were going to do a big monthly shop 50 miles away. So there we are. Taken a local house. Not spending any money locally if they can help it. No kids for the local school.

But the best bit was still to come.

They were very pleased that they had found out where the farmers met because they thought farmers were appalling people who were cruel to animals, polluted rivers, damaged the environment etc.

As soon as they settled in, they were going to form a group to act as watchdogs on local farmers.

Not content with moving into the area for a peaceful retirement in lovely countryside, they wanted to act as some sort of Green vigilantes as well.

She went to the loo then.

Someone suggested that the best place for Londoners was somewhere "off". The husband beat a hasty retreat.

It's the same with any farm on the market. Most of them are being bought by asset-strippers, who sell off houses, barns, etc, with attractive bits of land attached. Eventually, the remaining land is sold off at agricultural value, usually to a neighbour. Everyone seems quite happy, but it's yet another farm gone.

Mick Jagger bought the last one. I hope he doesn't start drinking in our bar.

August 1989

Green stuff

Was it 15% that voted Green in the Euro election? I can't remember now, but, whatever it was, you can be sure that the two major parties will go all-out to woo these voters before the next general election. They're probably not all Green: they are mostly people dissatisfied with the two major parties and without a realistic middle-ground party to vote for.

As I said last month, I am worried that we will be on the receiving end of a lot of point-scoring. Just to help, there is a very small minority within our industry who have a totally irresponsible attitude to the way they conduct themselves as they go about their business. I was in Shrewsbury market three weeks ago, at the unloading bays for the cull cows.

A lorry backed up with water running – obviously fresh from the wash. The ramp was lowered to reveal the interior pristine clear. Standing in the middle of the lorry was an old Friesian cow, also pristine clean, having obviously been treated to the same pressure washing treatment as the lorry. She was shaking violently and refused to come out.

"Bloody old fool went down in there with some store cattle," said the owner as he passed by to fetch an electric goad. After liberal application of this, she came down the ramp, tottered 10 yards and subsided in a heap. Shrewsbury market is near a large housing estate; it was half-term; there were mothers and children everywhere.

A week later I was leaving a local pub at 11.30 pm after a particularly hot day. The pub is next to the market. There were about 200 lambs still in the pens; they were making a hell of a noise; they probably hadn't had food or water since early morning, and had nothing to look forward to other than a long ride in a lorry. It was not necessarily a farmer's fault, but the people who I heard complaining about it didn't necessarily know that.

This week a local farmer has been in court for ploughing up an ancient fort. I reckon by the next general election farmers will be as popular in society as Rottweiler-owning lepers. They might even give us bells.

October 1989

In the doghouse
We had one of those dairy inspections the other day.

I thought we were off to a bad start when the first words the chap said were: "Right, we'll have that dog outside for a start." (That was a bit of a blow because I'd been teaching her – the sheepdog – to put the units on.) But it's right enough. That's the way we've got to think in the future. We've got to think of our parlours and dairies as food factories and treat them accordingly.

Our parlour is about 10 years old now, and there are a few cracks and crevices about that need tidying up. I might go for putting fibre-glass on the walls and flat surfaces of the stalls. A local lad repaired our rotting mangers for us with fibreglass and made a hell of a good job of it. I might even put a permanent pump in for washing out. One problem with our parlour is the large surface area and the time it takes to wash out.

Food and health scares are big news at the moment, and, as an industry, we must be beyond reproach. We must seek to continue improving our cell count position. (Still no option with NMR.) It is all very well doing enough just to get by, but standards will continue to tighten. It's far better to keep quietly in front than have someone pushing you from behind.

Top marks

One aspect of the current food scares that intrigues me is the position taken by many environmental health officers, that present laws are sufficient, but that they lack the manpower to enforce them.

I see quite a lot of game processing plants these days. They are subject to periodic inspections by health officers and obviously they must pass to stay in business. But the game business suffers from horrendous seasonal gluts - especially pheasants at the end of November.

Most of the game processors I know are constantly seeking new outlets for their produce. The one they all want to crack is access to the national multiple stores. But before their produce is accepted they are subject to inspection of their premises by the potential buyer.

The hygiene criteria insisted upon by these stores are far stricter than those required by the Government. A case of the food industry setting the standards and legislation following behind? The processors that are accepted by the multinationals consider it to be a considerable feather in their caps. Those that are accepted by Marks & Spencer are referred to with a reverence normally reserved for folk heroes.

So how many of us would pass the test if the man from Marks & Spencer opened our doors on a surprise visit?

It could come: the eventual buyer insisting on his own

production criteria and the MAFF inspector insisting on minimum requirements.

November 1989

I have bought three Texel tups at sensible prices. The two-year old is a very good sheep and was very cheap considering the trade.

(As is the way with tups, the bugger tried to commit suicide in the dipping bath yesterday. My son bought him back from the dead with skilful manipulation of his ribcage with his size 10 Noras. In the past he would have probably given him the kiss of life, but he's courting pretty steady at the moment.)

Lambing time could be very interesting next year. The farm where I run my sheep on grass-keep has gone in for free-range billy goats.

I think it started off as an attempt to fatten unwanted billy goat kids from a goat milk farm. The idea ran out of steam when the possibility of any profit disappeared, and they were turned out to grass.

Have you ever seen 15 billy goats sitting on a corn drill, none of them touching the floor? A very fine sight.

Anyway, these goats have been trying to have their way with my ewes all summer. I don't know if they were successful or not, but their equipment looked to be in very good order.

December 1989

We usually have a bit of banter around the inseminator's car while he prepares his straws. There was more than usual yesterday as there were six cows to serve. (That's what is technically known as an orgy).

The banter centred around how many of the six he would get in calf, and, if he was successful, which cows would eventually have which calf, as we were using four different bulls.

Ken ignored us completely whilst he prepared his different straws. Finally, when he had finished these preparations, back came his riposte:

"I was on a farm last week," he said, "and they reckoned you were either the worst or the unluckiest farmer in the world, because something is always going wrong and you are always whingeing about it in *Dairy Farmer*."

(An avid reader of *DF* is Ken – ever since I said he could only get a cow in calf if there was a full moon.)

A riposte indeed: one that set me back on my heels.

Ken went off with my son to get his cows in calf, and I jumped into my "new" three-year-old van to go collecting game. I drove very gently down our lane.

I had never dreamt that someone would see me as a whinger. I had always thought I was very cheerful. I know that I always seem to have a lot of fun. This was certainly food for thought, and I have thought about it quite a lot since. Although I have never seen my space in *DF* as an opportunity to catalogue my woes, the one thing I have very carefully avoided has been to parade my successes. In no way have I wanted to be seen as someone on an ego trip.

I had reached this basic conclusion by the time I reached the main road at the bottom of our lane.

I turned the steering wheel gently to the left and started off on my journey. Just as gently, the van carried on over the grass verge and into the hedge, the steering wheel spinning freely in my hand. By the time Ken caught up with me I had found that the main shaft between steering wheel and steering box had snapped through. (Subsequent enquiries revealed that all the vans of this type had been urgently recalled because of a design fault in the steering –but the computer, bless him, had missed mine).

At this time of year the van does about 1,000 miles a week, much of it on motorways with plenty of welly.

As I said to Ken, I might still be the worst farmer in the world, also possibly the luckiest.

The Nineties

April 1990

Blood pressure

I hadn't expected nitrate levels in water supplies to affect me particularly. I certainly hadn't expected them to cost me any money. We have always used a hosepipe to wash our parlour out. The water pressure has just about been adequate – not brilliant, but adequate. We recently suffered a drop in pressure, which put 10 minutes on the job.

I saw one of the local water Board engineers the other day, and he told me that our local supply was above the EEC nitrate levels, so they are having to pump water in from another area to mix with it. That is why the pressure has dropped, and he offered no possibility of it ever improving.

At the moment I am looking at pressure washers. There's always something ...

Dolce vita

I spent three glorious days in Italy with the rugby club in the middle of February. I don't know any Italian, but a friend of mine (or I used to think he was a friend) was in Italy in the war. I asked him if he remembered any Italian.

He only remembered one phrase, and he taught it to me. He couldn't remember what it meant but reckoned they used it quite a lot. I used the phrase for two days, and the results were very disappointing. I eventually found out it meant: "Come out with your hands up".

June 1990

I meant to tell you this last time, by my contribution was written in such haste (I expect you noticed) that I forgot. I must have had a busy week on the farm. "About time, too," I hear you say, echoed by my wife.

Towards the end of the last quota year we were all awaiting the allocation of an extra 1% quota from Brussels. This would have removed any likelihood of a national excess and consequent penalties. So there we all were, milking away as if there was no tomorrow, when suddenly everything was thrown into chaos because the Government wanted to allocate a percentage of the 1% to new entrants. As this proposal took quotas past the date when they are supposed to finish, Brussels vetoed the scheme, and for two or three weeks everything was in limbo.

The situation was eventually resolved, but whilst the deliberations were in process I received a photocopy of a memo from the Agriculture Department of my bank to their branch managers.

I don't know why I'm telling you all this. When my bank manager reads it, he'll have me taken out one morning and shot.

Anyway, most of the memo was concerned with the current position, the likelihood of penalties and so on. Down at the bottom in the small print was a suggestion to bank managers that where their clients were seriously over-quota they should encourage them to buy in quota. Fair enough in itself, but the last sentence was the most interesting.

"Your co-operation in this matter should provide an excellent opportunity to take a charge on the whole of you client's quota."

There are some rascals about, and they're not all foreign are they?

Mad policy

Since I last wrote I have had my first and second case of BSE. Once you have been involved, you have more set views on the whole business.

The Ministry seem to have based their tactics on the premise that the affected cattle are those that were fed offal produced when the processors were allowed (by the Government) to lower the temperatures at which they worked. (The cynic in me feels that because the fault can be laid on the Min of Ag doorstep that is why they increased compensation to 100%.)

They are hoping against hope that the disease does not pass from cow to calf and that the number of cases will reach a peak and then fade away. On dairy farms throughout the country there is a vast number of heifers out of affected cows. They are, in most cases, readily identifiable. A movement ban should be placed on them (fully compensated) so that their progress could be readily monitored. A proportion could be removed regularly for post-mortem testing. This would be a positive move rather than the "wait and see" approach.

A fish called ...

That will do for this month. I'm off to the pub now, and then I'm going to the fair to see if I can win a goldfish for the drinking trough in the collecting yard.

The last one from the fair lasted three years and grew to about a foot long. It got so tame that it would tug at your sleeve as you walked by the trough.

It died last summer. There was a cow bulling and it got overexcited and jumped out onto the floor.

July 1990

Yarn for spinning

Good story in the pub last night.

A friend of mine was shearing last week. He was approached by neighbouring smallholders to see if they could bring their two yearling ewes to be shorn.

When I say smallholders I mean "Good lifers". Not to be derogatory in any way – but we all know what we're talking about now. Anyway, Mary and Ivy duly arrived for shearing, Mary and Ivy being the two ewes.

Mary was shorn first amid much soothing talk and laying on of hands whilst she underwent this traumatic experience.

Now it was Ivy's turn.

"Be careful with Ivy, Mr Jones, we think she's in lamb, Mr Jones?"

"No, I don't," came the reply, "and what's more, I don't think she'll ever have one."

"Never have a lamb, Mr Jones? Why ever not?"

"Well, you see this little lump here in the middle of her belly? ...Well, that's where she pees. When sheep pee there, they're not girls; they are boys."

After shearing, Mary and Ivor were put back in their little trailer to go home. What's more, I suspect Ivor will live happily ever after.

December 1990

I've been thinking about milk bottles lately. I've been thinking about them since last Thursday, in fact.

My interest was focused even more sharply this morning I was driving back from a farmers' meeting in Glamorgan, and I was a bit dry. A bottle of milk would have done very nicely at about 5.30 am.

All this interest was sparked by the weekly visit to the pub by the local milkman. He calls on Thursday nights to collect his money. He always stops for a pint. (Well, he can afford to, can't he?) I asked him how much a bottle of milk costs these days. I was amazed to hear that he was charging 32p. (Mind, he does throw in the local gossip free.)

I hadn't really thought about the price of a doorstep pint recently, but had assumed it to be about 26p. Others in the company wanted to know how much I received. Sensing a sympathetic audience, I knocked a bit off and said about 60p a gallon. As his customers, they were all quite indignant, and he finished his pint and slunk off into the night leaving me to soak up the sympathy.

That was why a bottle of milk has been in my thoughts.

January 1991

The turkeys have been pecking the putty out from around the kitchen windows in preparation for another break in, so I've put some Christmas music on and they're now keeping their heads down in the buildings somewhere.

There are huge sieves fitted in the sewage plants to remove most of these "impurities". The film showed them (the sieves) being winched out before they were cleaned off manually. And a very fine sight they were too. As one of the men engaged in clearing them off their debris said, "Ladies' tights are hard to get off." But I already knew that.

March 1991

It's 9 February, and the phrase of the day is "chill factor". It's minus 6 outside the kitchen door and there's a cold easterly wind blowing. Siberia could quite easily be in the next parish by the feel of it, instead of thousands of miles away.

I mention 'chill factor' because it really is the week's "in" phase. The weather forecasters are using it all the time. It's not something we farmers are really aware of: chill factor. Our team would probably be "out of the wind".

It's why the ewes spend the night along an appropriate hedge; why we put bales and other wind breaks out in the field for the lamb; why we go around the corner for a natter.

It's why an old chap who used to work for me used to say it was bad weather for farm workers' eyes.

He reckoned the men would all find some excuse for doing some job around the buildings to get out of the wind. The eyes would suffer from peeping through cracks in the boards to see if the boss was approaching.

There is another sort of chill factor, one that can occur at any time of the year, but it's usually on Saturday nights in this house. You take your shoes off, you creep up the stairs, no lights on, into the bedroom, start to take your clothes off very quietly, and then just as you are taking the first leg out of your trousers, crash, over you go. The light comes on and things can then get very frosty.

Suffering Masses

After my comments last month about the state of Welsh rugby and my optimism at the time – a short explanation.

Everyone knows that in England Rugby Union is a middle-class sport. Everyone knows that in Scotland Rugby Union is a middle-class sport. Everyone knows that in Wales Rugby Union is a working-class sport.

Everyone knows that the working class suffer most in a recession.

April 1991

It's Saturday 2 March. I'm having breakfast in a small hotel near the centre of Paris. On the menu; croissants, chocolat, and to read, *Le Figaro*.

There we have it, on page 10.

"La maladie des 'vaches folles' signalee en Bretagne ... Une vache laitiere frisonne de cinq ans en est morte ... C'est le premier cas declare dans notre pays."

I'm over here making an indepth study of French dairy farming on behalf of this magazine (all expenses paid by the editor). The other contributors to this magazine don't go to as much trouble as I do.

There are probably those amongst you that don't have the benefit of an education in a good Welsh grammar school behind you. For you, a translation.

"Gosh! Mad cow disease, it is discovered in Brittany ... A milking cow, Friesian, of five years old, she is dead ... For France it is the very first case discovered."

This last statement contains a subtle double-meaning which would be lost on most of you. What the writer really means is "For France it is the very first case we have admitted to; all the other cows that have had this disease were diagnosed to have magnesium deficiency, straw poisoning and other innumerable problems, but I, the writer of this article, like most of my compatriots, am a stranger to the truth when it suits me." As you can see, the French can pack a lot of double-meaning into a sentence when required.

The article goes on to describe the disease and its symptoms, its link with the processing of offals for animal feed, and the devastating effect it has had on the British beef industry. The point about offals is particularly important in France when the possible transmission of BSE to humans is discussed. Very fond of your offal, the French, with 'triperries' everywhere.

The cow that died in Brittany poses enormous problems for the French Ministry of Agriculture, as she had the audacity to be actually born in France. This is explained away quite blandly in the article by the possibility that:

a) her mother was probably British and the disease passes from generation to generation – a fact that I didn't realise had been proved, or

b) she must have eaten some contaminated cattle food of British origin. (Very skilful passing the buck.)

In summary, it was suggested that the outbreak would be very limited and similar to the outbreaks in Ireland, where only 20 cases had been identified. Rascals, the French and Irish, where national interests are at stake – a fault to be admired in some ways. We in this country are so honest and straight in matters relating to the EC that it is usually to our own detriment. The herd in Brittany, where the cow she is dead came from, had been slaughtered (to stop the disease from spreading from cow to cow) and the farmer compensated by just over £1,000 apiece.

I bet it was a happy Breton who smacked his beret on his head and trotted off down to the café to tell his mates.

Beware of the apprentice

All about us are the signs of the recession: in our own industry and in the businesses of the people we meet every day. The other day I came across a new sign.

A friend of mine, who farms up in the hills near here, has a sheepdog that is a legend in its own lifetime for its ferocity. No pedestrian is safe within a 100 yards of his farm; it will, without any hesitation, bite you.

It is particularly famous for its brushes with authority, of which there have been several, people finding it very difficult to collect taxes and accounts if they can't get out of the car. This friend and I were discussing the economic situation in general, and he forecast very difficult times ahead. So difficult he had already taken steps in anticipation of the difficult times ahead. I was very interested to hear what these steps were, and he told me he had bought a new puppy dog.

He reminded me of the situation where the man collecting money was stuck firmly in his car and he was safely ensconced in his house – between the two was the ferocious dog.

"But how would I manage, Roger, if the dog died or was run over? I've bought the puppy dog so the older dog can train him to do the same job."

(He calls it a puppy dog. You should see him: he's well over 6ft and built like the side of a house).

"That way," he continued, "I am sure of one nasty dog to keep people away."

I saw him a couple of days ago and asked him how the puppy dog was getting on. "Very, very well," he replied. "He's bitten the postman twice already."

Rustic work

I am unrepentant about my remarks last month about newcomers to rural areas.

In a village near here, a carpenter has been turned out of his workshop because of the noise of his little 12" electric saw. He didn't use it all day every day; just when he needed it. The protests were precipitated by the artist who lived next door, who was backed up other relative newcomers.

It must be a great consolation to the residents of that village to know that if their kitchen door falls off next winter when there's a cold wind blowing, they can replace it with a very nice watercolour!

You mark my words, the same thing is happening with farming. If you milk cows near a village they won't allow you to milk before 9 am on Sunday mornings because of the noise of the vacuum pump.

We're probably all breeding the wrong cows for the future anyway. With slurry limitations and nitrogen limitations we should be breeding a cow that will produce 3,000 litres of milk off 3–4 acres of unfertilised land on once-a-day milking.

The chap who comes around here inspecting parlours and dairies is also looking for a cow that doesn't shit, so perhaps that could be incorporated in the breeding programme as well. Mind you, if we could get £1 per litre for the 3,000 litres it might not be so silly.

This will only be an interim phase because eventually all we'll be allowed to keep will be cardboard cut-outs of cattle and sheep. We'll be paid to move them about the field to simulate grazing groups of animals and we'll be paid to cut the grass around them.

Except on Thursdays. Thursdays will be your day off, the day when you travel to the nearest post office, which by then will be about 50 miles away, to collect your Giro cheque.

Oh, by the way, I don't want to hear any stories of any of you lifting sheep up by their wool. God may have put convenient handles on sheep but apparently we're not allowed to use them any more.

October 1991

A local lady – inevitably, a relative newcomer – appeared in the evening paper in front of a clump of nettles, which, she claimed, obstructed a public footpath. Farmers were to blame: they weren't going out regularly to clear nettles and briars from footpaths.

This was actually timed to coincide with a ramblers' publication about greater access to the countryside. The publication was called "We have a dream".

You can't believe it, can you? I bet that if Martin Luther King were still alive he would have wished he'd thought of that!

What our lady in front of the nettles failed to realise was that in the past there was never a need to cut nettles from footpaths because they were kept clear by people's feet. That they are overgrown now is because most of them are never used. They were not put there to provide recreation for a lot of fair-weather country people, but as a short-cut from cottage to farm, from farm to village, and from village to town, because most of the population had no other form of transport than their feet.

There's a bridge over a stream on our rented ground. I reckon it must have cost £2,000. But a sleeper would have sufficed because in the 27 years I have been here, I've never seen anyone use it.

I'm all for access to the countryside. Anyone who follows the country code can walk anywhere on this farm. But I actually think that some ramblers derive some perverse pleasure from finding a blocked footpath, and would be disappointed if they could not precipitate disputes with local authorities and farmers. I certainly don't see why I should go out cutting nettles and thorns every two weeks just in case someone decides to go for a walk every 10 years.

November 1991

Indolent – lazy, idle. That's how I feel today.

I knew how I felt. I just needed one word to describe it. It's nice to have the right word to suit the situation.

I remember an occasion in the pub.

A friend of mine was in a quiet mood one evening. He'd been shearing all day; now he was on his third pint, his pipe was going well and he was quiet and content.

A young lady interrupted his thoughts: "You're looking very soporific this evening, Frank!"

I ask you, soporific? In a public bar.

It had to be a newcomer. And it was.

Frank is very well read, so he know exactly what soporific means.

"No I'm not," he replied, "just …" well I won't tell you what he said next, but the word he uses most begins with f, regardless of who is listening. So he had the right word as well.

French leave

I've been to France again since I wrote last. Just for two days. A bit sad really: it was to call an end to my export business.

I should have stopped 12 months ago but I was quite proud of what I'd built up and I let my heart rule my head (not for the first time).

When I first started exporting game, there was a worthwhile margin between game values in this country and those in France. Over the last two years these have been eroded, mostly by game from eastern European countries, seeking foreign currency at almost any price.

My clients want to continue the friendship, visiting each other in alternate years, so who is to say it won't start up again in the future?

I always seem to learn something from the French. This year it was dipping lumps of sugar in brandy and eating them, and the advantages of diesel cars.

As regards the latter, as our families grow up there are more vehicles using the family petrol account. There is a very big saving to be made having your own tank of diesel and a diesel car. More miles per gallon and less gallons. I'm not going to rush out and change the car, but when the time comes …

The people I have been associated with are industrious and hardworking, which is a wonder with all that kissing and handshaking to do as well.

As I say, I always seem to learn something worth adopting. Diesel cars and kissing this time.

March 1992

Gypsy rover

We've got this dog. Well, we used to have this dog. His father was one of the best spaniels I ever had, and his mother a Jack Russell. He looked a bit like a small Bassett hound, only black and white.

I was down at the vets one morning, and, whilst waiting for them to sort out an injection for my turkeys, I read the small ads they have on the noticeboard.

I came to the lost-and-found section, and read of a dog found in the area. That sounds like our Fred, I thought. I hadn't seen him for a couple of days, but that was nothing new.

There's a weekend cottage a mile away down our lane. The visitors have a basket there for Fred. They bring him food every time they visit, and he goes there every day if they are there.

He'd always been a free spirit.

The girls at the vets phoned the number on the card, and I was directed to the local permanent gypsy camp. There I found chrome lorries, chrome caravans, chrome teeth and Fred. Very busy and very happy. I took him home, and he stopped 24 hours.

I went back to the gypsy camp, and there he was, though it's six miles away.

They want to keep him, and he wants to stay.

Dairy farming must have reached a very low ebb when even your dog prefers to go and live with the gypsies.

April 1992

Private eye

Someone suggested to me the other day that I had become neurotic about the pollution laws and agriculture's treatment compared with other industries. I now see that a weekly farming journal has taken up this theme as a regular feature. What you read in my column is at the very forefront of agricultural thinking! (If you believe that you'll believe anything.)

My latest little worry about privatised industries comes as the result of a television programme I saw recently. This highlighted the extra costs of servicing rural areas.

Services that are of particular concern here are power, water, post and telephone. It obviously costs more to provide these services to us rural dwellers than it does to a row of houses in the town. In an extreme example, the programme showed the cost of delivering mail to islands off the Scottish mainland. The cost was put at about £7 per item.

An accountant was quite adamant in his views. "If people choose to live in the countryside, then they must expect to pay the full cost of the services they receive. They will not, in future, be subsidised by the town dweller."

I will not be surprised to see the service industries bringing in tiered prices in the near future. The only muscle we have in the argument is that they invariable need to cross our land to supply others.

On open view?

I see that there is soon to be a ban on moving livestock in open-top transport. I'm all in favour of that.

I've often followed an artic load of lambs down a motorway at 70 mph on a cold day and felt sympathy for those on the top deck, and wondered what sort of chill factor they were having to contend with.

There is another important point here.

If you asked most people where meat comes from, they will say on a polystyrene tray, wrapped in clingfilm off a shelf in the supermarket. They prefer not to associate meat with animals – a head-in-the-sand attitude if you like – and they don't need to see animals in transit to remind them.

Landing in it

I always look forward to the spring. You shouldn't really, because you are wishing your life away, but you can't help it.

The best day of the year is the day the cows go out. I always look forward to that – this year more than usual.

The signal that the cows should go out is usually when the silage grab comes out with a forkful of stones.

There are no problems in this respect this year: the problem is overcrowded buildings.

I knew we'd have too many cattle for the buildings this winter and I arranged to rent some buildings a couple of miles away, to house and dry cows and heifers. Unfortunately, the owners of the buildings changed their minds in November.

Thank you very much, I thought, when they told me. It's a good job they weren't mind-readers.

Here we are: too many calves in the calf pens; too many heifers in the cattle yard; too many cows in the cubicles; about five cows lying in the … (whoops, nearly used the sh-word).

There are also two other species that have moved into the cubicles

A couple of years ago a friend offered me some of his son's tame pigeons for my game business: they were too pretty to tap on the head, so I kept them.

This autumn they all moved into the cubicles, and have been producing young since Christmas.

It is a perfect environment for bringing up a family. Plenty of places to build nests; nice and dry; nice and warm in cold weather when the cows are lying inside.

There is only one drawback. That is when it comes to training flights. For your young pigeon, about to make its way in the world, flying from roof truss to roof truss is OK. Landing on the floor is a very different matter. Cows may lie on you; tread on you; do the usual on you: you may be scraped away by an unobservant scraper driver.

Thus we come to the other species that has moved in to the cubicles. Sleek and shiny, stretched out at the front of the cubicles on the clean sawdust are the cats. For them, too, the cubicles offer a warm, dry environment. For them, there is also another advantage: every now and again a nice, fresh, tasty pigeon wearing L plates will land beside them.

The cats have never had it so good. It's almost like Happy Hour at Sainsbury's as far as they are concerned.

May 1992

For those of us with nagging worries about our effluent control, a small matter of perspective. Everything in life is relative, so here's something to think about.

National Power and Powergen – those stalwarts of electricity supply – have contracted to buy £0.5 million tons each of a product called Orimulsion from Venezuela. This is a mixture of tars and heavy oils, and it is intended that it will be burnt in power stations in West Wales.

It is expected that, as a result of using this product, sulphur dioxide emissions in the area will increase 10-fold, though the two companies involved say it will have no significant effect on acid rain in Wales. It will be interesting to see if the Government stands by its claims on pollution control. Those of you planning a holiday in Wales will need to take some litmus paper with you to test streams and lakes before your children play in them.

Compared with pollution on this scale, parlour washings going down a ditch are about as significant as a little boy peeing off a bridge.

A very nice young lady from QCB has just called. She gave me a big smile and sold me some semen from a bull called

Southwind: a bull with good type and good figures. Hers weren't bad either.

July 1992

Serious crimes?

Friday morning and it's market day in our local town. The market is quiet at this time of year – about 1,000 lambs at the most.

At the cross-roads outside the town, the forces of law and order set up shop: two officials from the department of transport, one official from the trading standards department and a local policeman.

They are there because it is market day, and it is farmers that they are interested in. When the market is over and the farmers have gone home, then so do they.

It's a good day, and local residents can sleep easily in their beds at night. Brought to book are two farmers using red diesel in their Land Rovers and one with a dirty trailer. Serious stuff!

On Friday night in the same town there will be about six youths selling drugs to young people. No law and order about now. In the hills above the town is a favourite camping place for hippies and New Age travellers. There are a lot of them camped on lay-bys around here, hoping to get up into our hills.

No checks for them for red diesel and roadworthiness.

In some ways I hope they succeed in getting up in the hills. It will give the police something better to do.

Barking up wrong tree

I have a very great admiration for people who have simple ideas that make money. Here are two examples.

One is the simple idea of putting spring water in bottles and selling it. I really like the fizzy sort.

A friend of mine used to drive a skip lorry. He emptied the skip at a place where they bottled this carbonated water. He used to bring me lots of it. If the packaging was damaged, they'd put it in the skip, bottles intact.

The other simple idea is the practice of putting tree bark on flowerbeds to stop the weeds growing.

Years ago they used to dump the bark in quarries. Now they sell it.

However, my admiration is tinged with envy. I cannot bring myself to buy either product.

Over the years, I have made several attempts to create what I have optimistically called shrubberies. The motive has usually been to reduce the areas of grass I have to cut in garden and yard.

The enthusiasm has usually waned as I discover the price of shrubs.

These "shrubberies" have become wild, neglected places – full of docks and nettles, and a sanctuary for fornicating cats.

January 1993

Passing inspection

The man who comes round this area, inspecting milking premises, is legendary.

He now has a new ploy: you get the notification letter about his visit the day after he calls.

He knocked on our door yesterday at lunch time, just when David and I were stretched out in the chair making very close inspections of the inside of our eyelids.

We came off better than we thought.

"Mend the dairy door." (A piece rotting off the bottom.)

"Mend the parlour door." (The bull had tried to force an entry.)

His parting shot?

Indicating our tame pigeons lined up on the roof of an adjacent barn:

"Don't let their numbers increase any more."

I've delegated all three jobs.

The first goes to the carpenter, the second to the blacksmith, the third to the cats.

September 1993

Our story today begins with my recent visit to the Royal Welsh Show.

I have clear memories of my day out. Someone like me, who goes weeks at a time without going off the farm, can always remember a day off. (If you believe that you will believe anything.)

The day got off to a good start. I went with my friend Kevin, and we were using his car, his petrol and his membership tickets.

Our first call was the MMB stand.

There we met my friend Tom Jones. (No, not that Tom Jones. This one is Board member for North Wales.)

Tom was in good form, having just been re-elected to the Board.

Tom Jones disappeared and came back with South Wales Board member Roger Evans.

Roger and I are often confused. (Well, I'm confused most of the time. What I mean is that we are often mistaken for each other.) Still, we had never met before.

Roger told me what a setback to his life and career it was to have the same name as me. Such a setback and liability that he was seriously considering changing his name by deed poll to a name less well known and of lower profile within the dairy industry: something like Richard Smith.

Biggest topic of conversation at the show was maize. It seems that everybody has a field, and everyone was amazed by how much it had grown recently.

The conversation usually went like this:

"How's your maize doing?"

"All right."

"How high is it?"

(This was the crunch question. Everyone I met had maize a foot higher than mine.)

"Up to my waist."

"Oh. Mine's up to my chest."

And so it went on all day.

"How high's your maize?"

"Up to my chest." (Triumphantly.)

"Oh. Mine's up to my shoulders."

Whatever I said, theirs was a foot higher.

"How high is your maize?"

"Up to my knees."

That stopped them in their tracks. Who's going to say that their maize is only up to their dick?

By the end of the day there were people standing on chairs tapping their chests to show how high their maize was. I didn't let it worry me. I haven't got where I am today without being able to spot bullshit.

Northern cross

Two items in the press have caught my eye recently. One in the national press; one in the weekly farming press.

The farming item was a letter from Northern Foods which basically warned farmers that they were wasting their time considering Milk Marque as a feasible prospective buyer of their milk because if MM was even 50% successful they would be prevented from trading by the Office of Fair Trading and by the EC.

This unfair situation would probably be brought to the attention of the OFT and EC by such public-spirited bodies as milk buyers.

This is so far from the truth that it's really a bit naughty.

Milk Marque will operate strictly under guidelines that will be approved by the OFT and Brussels before it moves one single litre of milk.

If MM moves away from these guidelines, it will be in trouble, but not until it does so.

Brussels and the OFT find the MM concept acceptable because there is no profit motive involved in MM. MM will be dedicated to moving milk quickly and cheaply from producer to user, and not trying to hold any of those users to ransom.

The irony of these threats is that while Northern Foods raise the spectre of OFT action, our ultimate customers – the supermarkets – are themselves attracting OFT attention.

The OFT suspects supermarkets of colluding on prices. (I warned of this last month.)

The OFT is interested to find that supermarket profits have continued to rise during the recession.

It is the supermarkets that will dictate what the dairy trade can pay us for our milk. Do you want the price of milk fixed by Milk Marque or by secret phone calls at the very top level of supermarket management?

I was also warned last month that the big supermarkets would be under pressure from the discounters.

An American supermarket wants to open a discount store near to the M25. There are three objectors to the planning application.

I shan't be handing out any prizes for anyone who guesses who the three are.

October 1993

We have a field of grass-keep, about a mile away, well known for its mushrooms.

It's a pleasant task, to go around the dry cows and heifers and pick up enough mushrooms for the family to have for breakfast. My liberal free-access opinion doesn't last long when I find someone else there before me!

Even worse are the crowds that flock to this area at August Bank Holiday time to attend a steam engine rally. I resent the crowded roads and the general upheaval that we suffer in this quiet backwater. It's a bit like Blackpool for two days, without the donkeys. But the very worst aspect of all is when I go to the pub on Saturday night and there's a complete stranger sitting in my seat, eating scampi and chips!

So, when it comes to the crunch, I can only pay lip service to public access. And there's us doing farmhouse bed and breakfast and relying on tourists for some of our income.

Tourism has been a bit better this year, after a couple of years in the doldrums, helped by catering for the guests at several local weddings. The only trouble with wedding guests is that you can book four young people in on Saturday night and eight come down for breakfast on Sunday morning. I'm thinking of putting a condom machine on the landing.

I see from last month's issue that my efforts are read in French toilets. I wonder if it's one of those with just a hole in the floor where you squat down and just when you think you've perfected the technique, you find that you've ...

No, it can't be one of those, you could never hold a magazine at the same time.

I was at a farmers' club dinner near Preston last week.

The first questioner must have been confused about my image as well. He asked me if I was more interested in sex or farming?

I thought he was joking. He probably thought he was being cynical. We were both wrong.

I was thinking about my image again yesterday while mowing the lawn.

What had happened to this man of the people, this champion of the underdog?

February 1994

Next generation

I've just had my first grandchild. A lovely little boy called Rhys Lloyd Evans. I've just been to buy him his first pair of wellies. The woman in the shop asked me:

"What age is the child?"

"Six days", I replied.

Tomorrow, he goes to see his dad play rugby (if the pitch dries out).

I don't believe in putting undue pressure on young people, but I think we may have another dairy farming rugby player in the pipeline.

April 1994

Foxes

We had the fox hounds round here last week. I am just amazed by the huge numbers of foxes that are caught and shot every year. One large shoot I visit had averaged one a day up to September last year and still they kept coming. Everyone reckons that the RSPCA release them out of the town. I did once see an RSPCA van pulling out of a wood. It was fitted out with cages inside and looked a bit suspicious – then again he could have just stopped for a jimmy. If we, as country people, were as sharp as we think we are, you would have thought there would have been firm evidence of this by now. Our local master told me that his hounds had caught several foxes with collars on and they certainly catch a lot more than they did 10 years ago, so where do they come from?

To return to the visit here, I used to think that there was no more stirring sight in life than three corgis in full cry after a rabbit. I've had second thoughts since. Two foxes chased by 30 hounds chased by three corgis is also a fine sight. As the whole procession came past twice (a sort of foxy lap of honour) I did wonder what would happen if the foxes caught the corgis up. Funny things animals. If I was a corgi and the hounds were about, I'd keep my head down.

Free range
The latest advert to catch my eye? Kerrygold Free Range Cheddar Cheese.

The story is about two Irish brothers who decide to become more efficient. They do their sums, make their plans and double their herd – from one cow to two!

The message is obvious: "our cheese is produced by contented stress-free cows that live in herds of two and graze lush fields where the grass is six feet high".

I have been to Ireland several times and I did actually see some very small herds of cows. I also saw some large herds crammed onto small paddocks with their tails cut off. Obviously Kerrygold don't use their milk to make cheese.

August 1994

I can't remember just which evening it was: I think it was during the week before the Royal.

There I was, in my favourite armchair, just after my evening meal. Outside it was raining, so there was no need to feel guilty about not mowing the lawn. As a friend of mine often says, the rain was doing more good than anything I could do.

At my left hand, my evening glass of red wine; at my right, the television controls, so I could turn up the volume if an item of interest came on the news.

Most of my attention was devoted to the evening paper, and whether I could sneak another glass of red wine.

But wait, what's this on the news!

A cow!

Turn the volume up quick. It's an item on the reshaping of the dairy industry and the demise of the MMB.

The reporter's introduction and the couple of farmers interviewed all have a familiar ring, and a sense of unease grows.

"How," the reporter asks, "will this affect consumers?"

I might have guessed. Here he comes: the champion of the consumer – the Robin Hood of the dairy trade – Chris Haskins.

"This is bad news for consumers. Farmers are banding together to form a monopoly to force up prices to the housewife."

Doesn't sound like a bad idea to me. Aren't monopolies those businesses where you get about £250,000 a year, and half a million when you retire, and your prices go up about 70% every five years?

The bit about farmers forcing up prices completely throws me. Only that morning I had received a letter from Mr Haskins' company promising me more money for my milk than the farmers' organisations.

We shouldn't underestimate Mr Haskins or anyone like him that can get an item onto the national news to put over their point of view. He bought the wrong horse and chose the wrong jockey, and now his career could be on the line. We ignore him at our peril.

I turn the volume on the television back down and decide to have the second glass of wine. If red wine makes you healthier because it makes your blood thinner, will I need to wear two pairs of socks in the winter to keep my feet warm?

I went to the Royal. The first time for many years. I went for the sole purpose of calling to see our editor David Shead, who has been unwell for some time and who is now back at work. Stoneleigh is about as near as he gets to us, so it was a good opportunity.

I am delighted to report that he looked well and was glad to be back at work. I think we probably underestimate his contribution to our industry. If you never went through the farm gate, you could keep completely up to date with our industry just by reading *Dairy Farmer*.

He obviously intends to adopt a healthier lifestyle. He was necking some sort of red wine down him whenever I was on their stand.

Welcome back, and good luck to him!

September 1994

Yesterday, the game season started with my first collection of grouse. It's a hard day. I leave home at 4 am, collect the grouse, bring them home, grade them and put them in the fridge. I had over 700 yesterday and I drove nearly 500 miles. You'll appreciate the next bit. You have your evening meal, and you're sitting in the chair watching television, wondering whether to go to bed at 8 o'clock or a quarter past and the missus says:"You never talk to me anymore."

January 1995

Dirty hands
Heard a good story on the radio the other day, one advantage of doing a lot of driving (about the only advantage at the moment) is you do get to hear some decent radio programmes. Radio Wales were interviewing a retiring bank manager, one who had spent all his working life in rural areas.

"What advice did you get when you took over your first branch with regard to your treatment of farmers?" he was asked.

"Look at their hands. Their hands were the most important thing, almost more important than the balance sheet. Hands didn't matter a lot, if they were blue-chip clients, but for farmers their hands were the most important thing."I was told to look for rough dirty hands, if they had rough dirty hands you knew they were hard working and they always had the benefit of any doubt. I've turned down good proposals because the applicant had clean, smooth hands." (Not many rough dirty hands around the table at Milk Marque Area Council meetings!)

Next we had an interview with a retiring farmer.

"What advice did you get, when you took over the farm, with regard to your performance with the bank manager?"

"My father told me that every day for three days before my annual visit to the bank, I should first rough up my hands with a matchbox, I should dip them in waste engine oil and rub it well in. By the time I went to the bank my hands would be very rough and very black. My father told me it was the first thing that bank managers looked for, to see if you were a hard worker."

Publicity

Consider for a minute the publicity given in the media to the transport of live animals to the continent and compare it to the coverage given to the ferry disaster in the Baltic. There's no comparison, no animals involved.

I've always believed if someone started to beat a dog on one side of the road and someone started to beat a child on the other, there would be more protesters around the person with the dog!

It must be nearly 20 years now since David and Annie Shead came here one Sunday to take a photograph of the "new" contributor to *Dairy Farmer*. I hadn't seen David that many times since, distance precluded that, but he was one of the nice men that you meet in life and I shall miss him.

February 1995

My subject this morning concerns an endangered species, a species under threat, a species under pressure. Farmers. People like you and me. We seem to have drifted into a role over the last few years where most other sectors of society seem to think we are "fair game" and it is open season.

My first little brush came a month ago. We were bringing 15 yearling heifers home to house them. There's a new house in the village with the inevitable open-plan garden, and the new owner (who is apparently a really nice old lady) had been moved in a week. The heifers spent several minutes on her newly sown lawn, despite our best efforts, and inevitably phone calls followed.

I didn't speak to her myself, I conducted a dialogue through the rest of the family. I (mistakenly, apparently) told them to tell her that unless she could prove negligence on my part, and that if I had taken reasonable precautions, I was in no way liable for any damage. She was soon quoting Acts at me.

Subsequent enquiries at my NFU office confirmed that I was indeed liable and if any damage occurs in the future she is ready to take action.

It just seems so wrong. I wonder for how many hundreds of years people have been moving stock through our village. This lady had only been there a week and effectively put a stop to it. (I'm the only one that does, or did it, anymore).

It's a funny old world. If you put stock in lorries they don't like it, if you walk them they don't like that either.

Twenty-years ago if I was driving a tractor through the village and I saw a stranger, I would slow down and have a good stare at them. Last week I drove through and saw 10 I didn't know, but they all seemed to know each other, and the buggers were staring at me!

May 1995

I spent a very pleasant afternoon tidying up some permanent electric fencing, with one eye on the cows enjoying themselves. Just when I needed him, along came Ginger to see what we were up to. He's worked here on and off for years, but never found full-time employment since the poultry plant closed in Craven Arms.

A hard working young man who would love to have a full-time job, he fills the three main criteria I look for in a young employee: he has a watch, he had a two stroke motorbike (very handy if you need some petrol for the chain saw) and he will catch hold of an electric fence to see if it's working when I tell him to, like now, and it was.

In our little local town, the pubs have gone down from seven to five in two years. If it goes on like this, in three years time we'll be drinking in the Spar shop, and they close at eight o'clock.

Increase

Meanwhile, the steady increase of town people living in the countryside goes on, every where, not just around here. They have a complete lack of understanding of the countryside, the weather, of rural life.

I can't remember the date of this incident, but I do remember quite clearly that it was the week when the world's eyes were on Holland and the dykes that were under threat. Rivers throughout the UK were on red alert for flooding. On the evening in question it was pouring down, to even the most casual observer it was bloody wet. At 9 pm the phone went: "Mr Evans?" the lady's voice said, "there is water running out of one of your gates onto the road." The tone of the call was indignant, I was clearly in the wrong.

You just have to stop and think about her motivation. She left me in no doubt that she would continue her telephone quest to discover the culprit (it wasn't actually my gate so presumably it wasn't my water). An extreme example, but typical of these people who live in our midst and who are such a pain in the arse.

The best news I've heard lately from conservationists is their suggestion that wolves should be released into the wilds of Scotland. At last they may go just one step too far.

I hope the wolves are released and I hope it is a complete disaster (I just hope that a child is not attacked). With a bit of luck conservationists will reel back under the criticism and their future plans may have a bit of balance.

Ramblers

We could do with a few packs of wolves around here, they might keep people in the towns or a least in their cars. It would certainly make the ramblers pick their feet up, give them less time to criticise. What other species could we re-introduce? I've got some mammoth embryos in the freezer, I might hatch some out under hen and loose them out on Bank holidays.

August 1995

A little story for those of you with imagination (it is true, mind you). They've recently opened quite a long bridleway across the Kerry hills in mid Wales. A party of young ladies set out one day on horseback (naturally) to enjoy this beautiful ride. Unfortunately, there was a stallion running with some mares on an open hill and one of the mares being ridden across this hill was in season. Apparently the stallion managed to service the mare while the rider was still in the saddle. I'm not saying another word.

October 1995

One advantage of living and working with nature (and I can't, just at this moment, think of any others) is that we can learn from what goes on about us.

There's been a daily lesson in optimism here throughout the many weeks of the drought. After morning milking our cows would clear up what was left of the wholecrop wheat silage on offer and then they would have a good feed of Tunnel Gold. The optimism would come after they, and I, had had our breakfast. I would go out and open the yard gate, their ears would go up and off they would go, full of anticipation and with a spring in their step, just as if it were the middle of May and there was lush grass everywhere.

Number 43 goes first, a Bear Path Fantastic daughter with most of our other Bears tight behind here. When I bought the Bear semen I saw a video on the bull and it said "follow the bear" which in our case is exactly what happens. So off they go, leaving me to reflect on their optimism.

In July they did have a poor crop of stubble turnips to go to, but as time went on the turnips actually went back as the dry weather tightened its grip. Towards the end I would move the electric fence and then wonder which side of it to put the cows. I eventually decided that the side to put them was the side where there was some shit.

Reflecting

But there wouldn't be much time for reflecting on the herd's optimism as they marched off into the distance, just time for me to scrape the yards and put some more silage out. They'd be back in an hour looking for something to eat.

I had to install a couple of those big black plastic drinking troughs to supplement the water on offer. We only have two troughs down the fields as there are several drinking places where the stream used to run.

In fact it was so hot and dusty on one occasion when I went to fetch the cows, that I took all my tack off and got into one of the troughs. And very nice it was too until the dog jumped in with me.

Lecture

I have an absolute dread of an antibiotic failure in my milk. Not because we are using a lot of antibiotics, just a fear of someone making a mistake. We keep a red aerosol marker in the parlour and any treated animal gets it, coming out of the parlour looking as if it has been attacked by graffiti. There's also a board on the wall where the treatments are logged – a simple, effective system.

Also in the parlour there is a green aerosol marker which we were using to identify some heifers that hadn't been branded. So one morning I was confronted with a heifer with a red cross on her but nothing on the board to tell me if she had been treated.

I kept her milk out of the tank, but enquiries revealed that she had received a green cross to tell me she was bulling, but subsequently it was decided they'd marked the wrong heifer, so the red cross was to cancel the green one.

I then delivered a lecture about the importance of red – for antibiotics and nothing else – and the dangers of making a mistake, rejected lorries and rejected silos and all that sort of stuff. I must have gone over the top with the sarcasm because all sorts of information is now appearing on the board and I can only assume that they are taking the piss.

It started off with udder grease treatment, then Uddermint treatment, before long I expect it to read like a ship's log, listing weather information, which field the cows were in and so on. I can put up with that as long as they remember red equals antibiotics, which equals milk for the cats and dogs.

Six months ago I met a very high-profile dairy farmer who told me he had been offered a new Mercedes car and £30,000 in his pocket if he could influence a large body of producers in his area to join a particular dairy. That is the sort of thing we are up against. Ignore it at your peril.

That little story alone should raise questions in your mind: how did your high-profile neighbour afford a new car and a new milking parlour at the same time? More important still, did Andrew Dare buy me my Transit van?

November 1995

Pub

There are some lorry drivers who get together in the pub every Saturday night. They drive their lorries all week, get home mid-day Saturday. Saturday afternoon they service their lorries. Saturday evening they relive their week, gear change by gear change in the pub and Sunday morning they're off again, off down the motorway of their lives.

Early in October there was a "Courtesy on the roads day", so to try to break up the interminable gear changes, blow outs and dropped pistons of their conversation, I innocently asked of them if they had been courteous on the roads that week.

Their conversation immediately became very animated and in no time at all they had reached the unanimous conclusion that on a courtesy scale of 1–10, bus drivers were firmly at the bottom, scoring about 1–2. They went on to say that bus drivers occupied a similarly low position in the social scale of life itself. This was apparently explained by the fact, something I was not actually aware of, that bus drivers - as a species - are, without exception, Bristol Rovers supporters. This in itself was considered sufficient explanation and they were all soon discussing tachographs. I was left to reflect on all this new information and to wonder if all these directors of Camelot who write nasty letters to the press about Milk Marque, are Bristol Rovers supporters as well.

A father and son had come to the end of one of a long series of arguments about the management of their farm. Once again, father had had his own way. He looked at his disgruntled son and said: "All right, if I gave you complete charge of this farm, what would be the first thing you would do?" Without any hesitation his son replied: "Get rid of you."

January 1996

Just when you think things can't get any worse, they do. My pub has closed. The full treatment, plywood everywhere. One of my greatest relaxations was to sit on my settle every Saturday night and watch the world go by.

That's three out of seven pubs closed in two years. I prefer a public bar to a lounge. You rarely find anyone to help you on the farm in a lounge. The trouble is, I can't get settled, I can't get backed into a corner and feel comfortable, I know just how a hermit crab feels when it changes its shell. I suppose I could always stay home and be miserable.

You should never say: "just when you think things can't get any worse, they do". What you have read up to now was written this morning while I waited for the effects of last night's drink to wear off. I blew some chestnuts up in the microwave, so I thought I'd leg it before Ann got up (this is Sunday by the way).

We went out to milk this afternoon and found a small heifer trying to have a big calf. Kevin got started on the milking and Sally fetched David (he lives five miles away) to give me a hand (he likes to try one on Sunday afternoons). We decided after about half an hour to call the vet (who was also trying one) and he decided on a Caesarean.

He was just making his first incision when Ann

announced that a neighbour had phoned to say that a heifer was stuck in a cattle grid on the grass-keep. Kevin and David went to the heifer and we continued the operation.

An hour later – and with a live calf – we went off to see how things were going at the grid. The heifer was out thanks to the efforts of the fire brigade, unharmed but shaken. David even had a lift home in the fire engine. An eventful evening.

Just as I gather these notes to put into the fax machine, I am told that leasing prices have collapsed, well gone down to 11p. If you were lucky enough to hang on to the very end, good luck to you.

February 1996

I send these notes to the editor written in my best longhand, which isn't very good. I bought some cheap A4 pads and can only say that my handwriting is appalling, the first time I get to read them myself is when they are printed in *Dairy Farmer*, which says a lot for the patience of Kathy in the office. So my New Year's resolution is to try to learn to use the computer and word processor that my daughter and daughter-in-law have in my office. I don't know how it works, although I can switch it on if someone calls and I want to impress them.

March 1996

I've always thought our use of minerals was a bit hit and miss. We've always sprinkled them on the silage and hoped everyone had their share. We've now gone onto liquid minerals that are introduced into the drinking water. We've got a sophisticated little pump that pulses it into the water as it is used. I know that cows can be very obtuse, but I think there's a fair chance that most of them have a drink of water every day.

The only question we had was where to site the pump. The minerals were too expensive to wash the parlour out with. I suppose that if I went far enough back up the mains, I could have put the village on it, no one would have noticed as our mains water is a disgrace. We get white scum in the kettle and so much chlorine in it I sometimes think it comes straight out of the swimming pool in Bishops Castle. We compromised in the end and the only group that is not on the system is the dry cow group (which I suspect probably need it the most). They drink out of the tank in the collecting yard, which is a large concrete vessel that apparently was used to soak straw in caustic soda during the war. The reason they are not on liquid minerals, is that there are six very fine goldfish living in this tank and we're not sure what effect the minerals would have on them. The dry cows will have to be content with mineral buckets until we find a new home for the goldfish.

Sitting here, day dreaming, I was thinking again about the snow last week. After we'd done the jobs and seen the milk tanker in and out, I had to pop into town. I'm always on about how many people have moved in, in recent years. That morning they were all on show. I don't think they can have seen a foot of snow before. All the locals were going about their business as best they could, in well-worn serviceable cold weather clothing. The new ones were all in brightly coloured ski clothes, like a parade from a catalogue, new gloves that they'd had for Christmas, camcorders and cameras over their shoulders and standing about in the middle of the road. I soon put the buggers back on the pavement.

There are myths, like the Loch Ness monster. There are legends, like King Arthur and Robin Hood. There are fairy stories, like the tooth fairy, and then there's the bloody penny. I've got my Milk Marque hat on now, (as if you hadn't guessed), well I haven't had it on for a long time.

The biggest problem that Milk Marque has at the moment is the misconception (we all know what misconception means don't we?) that everyone who sells his milk to someone other than Milk Marque, gets a penny more per litre. For some people there's more than a penny, but these people are in a minority. I've seen people's quality figures where they are desperately low on protein and fat and probably only get 21–22p/litre. Their litre is nowhere near Milk Marque's standard litre, or anybody else's standard litre. If they move to a liquid milk buyer, they will probably get

25p. There's no answer to that, some people call it the "white water" trade, but they're getting a bit touchy about that so I will call it 'whitish milk'.

It won't last much longer because the buyers of this product, who are mainly supermarkets, have become aware of it and they don't like it. It doesn't really make much difference to them, but they don't like the idea that they are buying milk that may be deficient in some way, especially in protein.

Some people leave for other reasons, but they don't always tell you what those reasons are, although they are quite good at making a few reasons up. They also are in a minority. For the vast majority of us, there is nowhere near a penny difference. We do a computer comparison when necessary and invariably, producers are annoyed at how close we all really are.

Contrary to popular opinion, there are not long queues of members waiting to leave Milk Marque. The battle for suppliers goes on, and why not? It keeps us all sharp. Dairies have become aware that having a large milk field of their own, their own supply base, enhances the value of their own company.

Milk Marque has quite a big milk field. It's worth a lot of money, I don't know how much, but I've got a share in it. It could be as valuable as my quota for all I know, I don't intend to give my quota to anybody, especially someone whose long-term aim is to drive down the price of milk.

To conclude the dairy politics, there is strong evidence in some areas that dairies are encouraging dairy consultants to take an anti-MM stance. Next time you are doing your costings and your adviser seems a bit uncomfortable on the kitchen chair, could it be because of the big wad of tenners he has in his back pocket?

My diversifying days have come to an end for another year and I'm back to being a farmer again. I'm having a bit of trouble with my back. I've forgotten where all the holes are in our concrete and I keep giving myself a nasty jar when I step in them.

I'm having a bit of a break at the end of the month. I'm

going to Ireland with Monmouthshire Grassland Society. I did suggest at yesterday's board meeting that the farm should pay all my expenses for this educational and cultural excursion. My idea fell on stony ground. Apparently (completely unknown to me) there's some rugby match on in Dublin while we are there.

April 1996

At about the time when conservation and green issues became the vogue, birds of prey were held up as the indicator of the state of the environment. Well, if the state of nature is reflected in these birds of prey, then nature seems to be doing quite nicely, around here anyway.

Buzzards and badgers

In the 30 odd years I've been here, I've never seen so many buzzards. There's even one lives around the yard. I don't like the way it keeps following me about. I expect they've cleared up all the wounded pheasants and have moved on to dead lambs and afterbirth. Come the spring and I bet there's quite a few young birds that will get munched up.

The last time we had the dairy inspector here, bless him, he condemned all my pigeons to death. They lived in the cubicles and he didn't like them shitting on the beds. (Good job he didn't spot the robin that lives in the parlour). I shot a couple with the air gun, but it didn't seem very sporting. Me with the air gun, the pigeons on the rafters and the cats waiting for a fresh meal below. No need to worry, let nature handle it, a goshawk has cleared out the lot.

Three cheers for badgers. Twenty years ago if you saw one a year run over on the road that was about the lot. These days I see about three a week. People tell me that there's a lot of TB in Herefordshire. People tell me that there's of lot of TB in Gwent. Coincidence?

Balance is the thing, be it buzzards or badgers. No use having buzzards everywhere and no song birds, no use having lots of badgers about at the expense of cows.

I enjoyed most of my trip to Ireland. For a week before I went everyone around here was going down with a nasty stomach bug. I thought that I'd missed it. I hadn't, it just waited until I got to Ireland. Not quite what you need when you are supposed to be necking Guinness all day.

That's all, what shall I do now? Outside it's still snowing, inside the women are making a wedding dress. Inside or out, neither is a fit place for man or beast.

May 1996

In my contribution last month, my handwriting was translated to "Three cheers for badgers", while it should have said "Then there's badgers". I can't read my own handwriting, so I shouldn't expect others to do it, but I only mention this because I know there are a lot of people who would decline to join in three cheers for badgers.

I've found out a bit more about badgers since last month. In Herefordshire for example, one of the counties I mentioned as having a TB problem, 65% of badgers caught are affected by TB. This compares with a national average of 25%. Surely this tells us all we need to know about the spread of TB in cattle. I am told, by an authoritative source, that the problem is spreading rapidly: "It will soon be affecting you."

Badger lovers seem incapable of taking a balanced view of this. I'm no badger hater, but I soon could be if my cows started to go down with TB – they've got enough problems.

A friend of mine said I'd have plenty to write about this month. The trouble is that as I write all the details have not yet emerged.

One aspect has troubled me. I hadn't realised, until this latest crisis, that treated offals were still being used in pig and poultry rations. I was appalled at the naivety of this. This explains one particular aspect of BSE that had concerned us all, the appearance of BSE in some younger animals which in theory had not been exposed to contaminated feed.

Assumption
The only safe assumption is that feeds were contaminated

and that we could be infecting our stock even today. I spent about four days wondering if all my older cows would have to go in a compulsory cull, we would have lost 38 to that – it's not a pleasant feeling. Kevin, who helps us at weekends, said he wouldn't help to load them, David said he wouldn't either – thank you very much.

Last Sunday morning, after my customary Saturday night at the pub, Ann said: "You were pissed last night."

Any wonder? The same thing happened again this week, only I think that was more to do with a new barmaid who thought that a white wine and soda consisted of half a pint of wine and a teaspoonful of soda.

As I write, we await further important announcements, so there is little point in further conjecture here. I have assumed for years that we, engaged in agriculture, had little political power, because, compared with the continent, we were numerically insignificant in voting numbers. That, to my mind, has now changed. What we have seen in this beef crisis is the sheer scale of our industry and the knock-on effect – if the farming boat starts to rock, all the other boats on the pond start to rock as well.

Milkings record

In March, I organised a dinner for Milk Marque members in my area. I thought we'd done well so far, why not celebrate it? I think it was a good do, everyone seemed to enjoy it. Andrew Dare was our guest speaker and everyone had an opportunity to meet him.

Unfortunately one incident overshadowed the rest of the evening. One of my friends chose this occasion to announce that he had just done 85 consecutive milkings.

Well, talk about a show stopper, everyone agreed that this must be a world record. Its not everyone that becomes a legend in their own lifetime. Like the England two, that's the two knock-ons that preceded Rory Underwood's try against Wales that the referee chose to ignore because all those people enjoying corporate hospitality, and probably their first live rugby match, expected to see Rory Underwood score a try – that's what they'd paid for. Heinz 57, self explanatory, and now the Watkins 85. It makes you feel quite humble to be present when history is made.

Burial

Some friends called the other day. We hadn't seen them for some time, she was saying that her father had died recently and that they had buried him in the garden. I was quite taken with the idea. Apparently it's quite legal and easily organised.

There's a nice cedar tree in our garden, one of my favourite trees, and there's a nice view. I never fancied ending up in a church yard next to a lot of people I didn't like, or as a plate on a wall at a crematorium among a lot of people I didn't know. Under the cedar tree has a lot of attractions, I could keep an eye on things, do a bit of haunting. But, could I trust the family not to put me in the slurry pit?

June 1996

Its been a busy social month as well. First there was the Rugby club dinner, my job that, guest speakers this year Jack Rowell and Martin Bayfield, two big buggers by any standards. It was all organised in a bit of a rush so I had to make do with them. Next year I'll go back to proper speakers from South Wales.

Then there was the wedding, last Saturday. Too many farmers invited for my liking. I was hanging gates and tidying up fences for a fortnight. The place was stinking of creosote, and so was I. And now I can't find a decent piece of string anywhere. They phoned me up from the church and said that as my daughter was getting married there, perhaps I would like to make a donation towards repairing the church. I told them I'd pay for all the repairs if they'd pay for the wedding.

There's one thing I do miss now my daughter has gone, I don't have such a wide choice of shampoo when I go for a shower. I could get in the shower and shampoo for dry hair, greasy hair, improve the health of my scalp, condition it and bring out the highlights. I still have a choice, but I have to leave the bottles upside down to achieve it, who knows what I'll be on next week. Probably Fairy Liquid.

July 1996

Reminder

I did bottle out a bit on my annual reminder to the inhabitants of the village, that they live in a rural area. We had 27 cattle to take through the village, but it was going to be even more difficult than last year. A new development in an old orchard had left another 50m of unfenced road.

I compromised by putting electric fence posts and string along all the vulnerable places. It was worth the effort. The cattle went through as good as gold and I had the added satisfaction of scoring a few verbal points with all the householders who came to ask why I was putting string across the front of their gardens.

There was an old vixen hanging around here all spring. In the end I put the shotgun in the airing cupboard in case I had a chance to shoot her. Having your shotgun in a gun cabinet up in the attic doesn't exactly leave you quick on the draw. Well, fair's fair, she had taken our only three hens just as they started to lay again. And if a hen can't live and lay in the cubicles unprotected, what is the world coming to?

Naturally as soon as I had the gun handy, I never saw her again, but I did track her down with my nose a month later. The cheeky bugger had laid down and died in a corner of the cubicle shed.

Posturing

Last week on the news, the Government was bringing in a law to prevent farmers from storing banned feeding stuffs on their farms. Political posturing it maybe, but what a disgraceful thing to say. I was talking to someone in the meat trade last week. He reckoned that the renderers in this country – who are apparently 80% Dutch owned – are on a sort of go-slow in their responses to Government urgings to help in the BSE crisis.

By this means, they are increasing the backlog of work simply to screw more money out of the system. If you cast your minds back, it was the renderers who screwed it all up in the first place.

On the same theme, gossips and rumour has it that some of us have been feeding our young calves milk powder containing animal by-products until quite recently. The excuse is that technically, they were non-ruminants. Nice to have another six or seven years of BSE cases to look forward to.

Every month there is news of a new genetic engineering breakthrough. The latest is that animals can father human beings. I thought they already were, certainly vice versa.

A lot of people have said they are taken with my idea of burial in the garden, or on the farm. We've now done two weddings here and everyone says they were good 'dos'. The next big 'do' we have here will be my funeral. I've chosen my spot in the garden and it will be a good day out. I know my wife is really looking forward to it.

August 1996

Contractor

My contractor told me that he'd had to mix the kale seed with sawdust to get the right seed rate, so we are assuming that the kale seed settled out in the hopper and that the last patch was only drilled with sawdust. There's not much I can do about it now, it probably won't look as bad when the sawdust germinates.

All our in-calf heifers and dry cows are away from home during the summer and we bring them home about a month before calving. We've had two heifers at home waiting to calve, and as I looked at them each day I looked at one with disappointment and one with trepidation.

The disappointing one is too small, in poor condition and has a brown, copper-deficient coat. The other one is something else. She's always been wild. Her mother was just the same. When she was away on keep last summer, she roamed at will whenever she was bulling, clearing any fence with ease. She fell in love with a neighbour's Limousin bull running with his suckler herd and even when he'd got her in calf, she still insisted on staying with him.

When the suckler herd was removed, she was distraught. She went walkabout looking for them. I am currently in negotiations with Walt Disney for the film rights to this poignant love story.

We didn't see her for a month as she roamed the parish. Everyone knew her, mainly because she had an anti-suckling device in her nose, I hadn't mentioned that had I? Reports would come back, mostly in the pub on Saturday night: "I see that heifer of yours is up on the top with Jones' sheep," I would be told.

Eventually she came home and settled down and that's where all the trepidation has come from. But you've probably guessed the rest, she comes in the parlour like a lamb, is an absolute sweetie to milk, and we've taken the spikes out of her nose and everyone's happy. You've probably also guessed about the poor heifer as well, she turned out to be a miserable little sod, always knocking the tack off and fidgeting about.

Last month I said that agriculture's high fliers wore Semex caps and John Deere overalls. It wasn't my idea, I pinched it off Terry Morgan, but yesterday a new Semex cap arrived in the post. One hour later, a new pair of wellies arrived by van to replace a pair that went missing on an expedition for *Dairy Farmer*. They're a bit embarrassing really as they are the yuppie wellies with buckles on the side.

So, I've got a new cap and new boots, but there's still room for new overalls in the middle.

September 1996

A few days ago a young cow developed quite a nasty summer mastitis. She was very sick with it and started calving eight or nine days before she was really due. She eventually produced twins, a normal size dead bull calf and a tiny weak heifer calf. I said to David that it was a pity it hadn't been the other way around. I would never have said that 12 months ago. It just shows how BSE has influenced our daily lives.

We hear a lot, these days, about producing what the market wants. This applies to almost everything in every industry and we pay lip service to it as milk producers. The reality is somewhat different. Our customers apparently are short of protein. We as dairy farmers, black and white breeders in particular, but other breeders as well, have been breeding away from market requirements for the past ten years.

Just to finish on a cheerful note, I was talking to a farmer the other day. He was in no doubt that the future for all of us was grim.

"You mark my words," he said, "over the next few months they'll find BSE in pigs, poultry, eggs, potatoes, milk and everything we eat. In no time at all we'll have nothing going out and nothing coming in.

"We'll be living hand to mouth on what we can produce on our farms. It'll be the 1930s all over again, subsistence farming at its worst, spending most of your time with your arm down a rabbit hole looking for your Sunday dinner."

November 1996

It is such a shame that deregulation has meant the end of innovative adverts such as the dancing milk bottles. A friend of mine visited the US last year and he talks about first-class adverts, many using famous models, that have made a real impact on milk sales and increased the consumption of liquid milk.

I wouldn't mind paying a small levy on my milk to sell it as a liquid drink and most producers I speak to, feel the same. Most areas of the trade are trying to prepare us for an expected steady decline in milk prices and for obvious reasons, do not want to spend money on anything that would buck that trend.

Photos
We had a really lovely break in Oban. The holiday photos came out well, especially the ones of my friend and I consuming large quantities of oysters down by the harbour, with a big crowd of people watching us. Apparently there was one photo we'd not seen because last week I had a very nice letter from Strathclyde Police. They hoped that I'd come back again sometime, and when I had a minute to spare would I mind sending them my driving licence and £100!

Financially, we've had several disappointing years. All down to the cost of leasing quota. In retrospect, I know that I should have tried to buy quota a few years ago, but there's no mileage in being self-critical about a wrong decision like that. My future budgets will involve milking the quota we actually have and if we can acquire extra quota (leased or bought) in any particular year at sensible prices, I hope to have the heifers due to calve and the crops in place to feed them.

December 1996

We always used to be worried about overfilling our milk tank at this time of year. This year, milking to the quota we have, rather than what we have leased, we are able to go on alternate day collection with our existing tank. Alternate day has its advantages: I overslept last week – really overslept as in 7am – it was some comfort to know that the tanker wasn't calling that day and the driver wouldn't be able to tell all my neighbours about my little difficulty.

Milk Marque tankers are starting to carry names. The names are supposed to represent National Heritage sites, though one tanker in the Oswestry area, apparently had to have its name changed because of an unfortunate local coincidence.

Our tanker is called Bessie Surtees which doesn't ring any National Heritage bells with me, so I can only assume that it is the name of the driver. When he first came round here he said his name was Clive so he must have changed it; it takes all sorts.

I heard a story the other day about someone who had bought a load of biscuit waste for his cows. Having a look through it one day, as you do, he noticed some broken dog biscuits. He was able to identify the make, so he went out and bought some. No prizes for guessing that the dog biscuits contained all the bovine bits and pieces that are not supposed to be available to ruminants anymore.

I heard also that there is a product available on the market called processed grain. It sounds innocuous enough – almost wholesome. I was told it was a by-product of the poultry industry. How would the poultry industry have a grain product to spare? But processed grain it is, it is processed by passing it through chickens (What the more technically-minded among you would call chicken shit).

January 1997

I wouldn't mind £1 for every time someone has told me recently that antibiotics in food is the next big scare waiting to happen. National newspapers are apparently already sniffing around the food industry, looking for a story. I have even heard it suggested that some dairy companies have a cavalier attitude to antibiotics and are not as scrupulous as they should be.

There are lots of stories about rogue teats and cows producing milk that will fail even after stipulated withdrawal periods are observed. I think a lot of dairy farmers have a mental block here. Ultimately, it's up to each individual to have his own testing kit and to use it as a routine.

The professional dairy farmer of the future will test every cow when she calves and every cow that has been treated before putting her milk into the tank. He will do it as routinely as he will put the bung in the tank before he starts milking. Failure to do either can be expensive and we've all forgotten the bung at some time.

There are no grey areas with antibiotics, we just have to be as near 100% on the ball as it is humanely possible to be, whiter than white you could say (and that's a fair mix of metaphors on a Monday morning).

Advertising
There's almost a paragraph in my dictionary explaining the meaning of generic, so I can only assume that they are not sure what it means. We hear the word quite a lot, generic advertising, or rather the lack of it, for milk. What it really means is dancing milk bottles and that nice milk roundsman encouraging people to drink milk. Since deregulation we haven't done any, and for a time I felt that people at all levels of our industry felt there was no longer a place for it.

Recently I have sensed a change in attitudes, at farm level and at higher levels. I actually think that if someone took the initiative that it would be better received than it was even 12 months ago. Even if it was only 0.1p/litre it would be a start, something to evaluate and to base future advertising policy on.

If you told the man from the Coca-Cola advertising office that you had a multi-million pound industry producing a drink that had been popular for thousands of years, but that you didn't actually spend any money on advertising it he just wouldn't believe you.

February 1997

We've suffered a bereavement since I last wrote. My scraper tractor died. I'd scraped half the cubicles and was going around the rest with a fork, tidying up, before scraping them as well. I'd left the tractor ticking over and it stopped. I'm no mechanic, but I knew from the way it ground to a stop, that it was finished.

A friend of mine had been visiting a relative in hospital. I asked how the patient was. "He's arseholed," came the reply. Next time you hear a hospital spokesman say someone is critical, you now know what they mean.

It summed up the state of my tractor – it was arseholed as well. And yet, I'm not too upset. I never really established a relationship with that tractor, she was using as much Easystart as diesel and the bitch let me down on a Sunday morning. A replacement took some finding, six days in fact.

Our other tractor won't go in the kennels, so we had to drag the muck out of them with the loader and bucket as best we could, it was a shitty sort of week. I bought the replacement unseen, it cost nearly twice as much as I expected, but it didn't sound too bad for a D reg. Trouble was, I didn't ask at which end of the plate the D came.

It was so cold yesterday that the new tractor wouldn't start. David said: "You take those four Limousin calves to the collection centre in my van and I'll see if I can get the tractor going." As we loaded the calves up, I enquired if the back doors of the van were safe. "They've never come open yet,"

David assured me.

About a mile from home I happened to look in the mirror and I saw this Limousin calf running along behind me. "I wonder whose calf that is?" I thought.

March 1997

I spend most of my life with my wellies on walking about in shit. This tends to make you a bit of an expert on the subject, so when someone stands up at a conference and supports the cause of low fat, low protein milk, you know that you've just stepped into some more crap.

Within the next three years, we will have to embrace the concept of world markets. In that market, a parcel of milk will be broken down into all the little bits and pieces that there is a market for. Protein will be standardised, ultra filtration will take place and there will be a market for every single fraction of that milk.

Designer milk

Designer milk is only a separator away and the successful players in the world market will be the ones who can place these components into highly profitable niches.

This talk of 3.70% fat and 3.00% protein is absolute crap. Your average litre of milk will be around 4.30% fat and 3.30% protein in five years' time because that's the sort of cows we are breeding now. If someone wants to reduce any constituent, he just takes out what he doesn't want and sells it somewhere else. To take this argument to some conclusion you could even say that the cow with the brightest future is a Jersey because her milk has so much more to work with.

I know a farmer, who, many years ago, would put a drop of hypochlorite into each of his milk churns on hot nights in the summer. Quite an effective way of stopping it going sour. We don't have to do that anymore with bulk refrigerated milk, thank goodness, and we certainly wouldn't be allowed to.

I think of this every morning when I stumble into the kitchen, release a tidal wave of barking corgis onto a sleeping world, and grab the kettle for that first important cup of tea.

The first water of the day from the tap stinks of chlorine, that's what reminds me of the hypochlorite in the milk churn.

The water board put chlorine in the water to mask its deficiencies. What chance you or I putting a jugful in the milk tank every day for the same reason? Hypocrisy, double standards, they abound everywhere.

I've had quite a good week this week, we're in the thick of the lambing, two lambed, two to go. I'm on my own in the house for a week which means I can read at meal times, choose the television programmes and I've left the wardrobe doors open all week. Tomorrow I'm off to Paris, apparently there's some rugby match on.

April 1997

If I carry on from where I left off last time, I was in Paris. A rugby weekend at my age is more about sightseeing and nice meals, rather than endless drinking and hangovers.

Our first day was spent sightseeing, we saw an exhibition of soft porn which was called the Picasso Museum and we saw the most remarkable shop. As only a few of us who read *Dairy Farmer* were lucky enough to go to a good Welsh Grammar School, I will translate the name of the shop for you: Shop for the destruction of undesirable animals.

Can you imagine the reaction to a shop like that in this country. The equivalent would be a pest control company and it would have exactly the same role, but they would be well out of sight. The French shop was up front, on a busy thoroughfare and had a very fine display of undesirable animals in the window.

From insects to foxes, rats, mice, birds you name it, it was there. They'd all been to the taxidermist, but it was a revelation. If such a shop existed in this country, you wouldn't be able to see the window for animal welfare pickets.

On the same sort of theme I remember Paul Lassman saying in a recent article that he had had a busy morning delivering calves and then dispatched the bull calves himself. I remember thinking at the time that I wouldn't fancy that job.

I was at a dinner a couple of weeks ago (more roast beef), and someone was telling me that their daughter had been in New Zealand and that in some areas they had pens at the end of their drives, and that they put their bull calves in the pen as they arrived. At some time during the day, the knacker man would turn up, shoot the calves and put them in his lorry. Can you imagine that in this country? A pen full of little Bambis bawling for milk, a pack of ramblers leaning over and letting the calves suck their fingers. Then this lorry pulls up and the driver jumps out. He'd probably have sunglasses, a macho moustache, denims, tattoos and a machine gun (Well, if you're painting a picture you might just as well splash a bit of paint about). What happens next would defy description, so I won't try.

This all begs the question, why are we, as a nation, so silly about animals? Using animals as a source of food is hardly a new concept. It isn't some new idea first seen on *Tomorrow's World* a few years ago. In fact, I can only think of one other concept that could be older, other being the key word.

I am convinced that we are as humane to animals as anywhere else in the world, yet we have a harder time from the general public than anywhere else. I always had a theory that if you took a dog and a child to a busy shopping centre and started to beat both at the same time, there would be more people trying to stop you beating the dog than the child.

I don't even like the idea of these pens for the calves at the end of the drive. I have an uncomfortable feeling that I would end up in there one day.

A few months ago I changed my car, I was looking for a low mileage economical diesel, but these are as rare as a modest England rugby supporter and I bought a 3-litre, 24-valve as a temporary measure. It has electric this and electric that, computers for everything, buttons everywhere. It's so complicated that I didn't even know how to switch the interior light on and can only achieve this by opening the door.

It broke down on me in Cornwall last week and I spent some time in a lay-by near Bodmin. It spent all day on a computer the next day while one computer tried to find out what was wrong with another, without any success.

Waiting about gives you time to think. I thought that 20 years ago someone would have blown some shit out of the carburettor and I would have been on my way.

I also thought how economical my car was when it was riding home on the back of an RAC lorry. And I thought that in the run-up to a general election, a few weeks spent on a lay-by outside Bodmin was not without its attractions.

May 1997

It hasn't been that good a time for me or the dog. We've got this bearded collie bitch, she's got to be the best dog I've ever had, and that's out of a lot of dogs.

She's not been on her full power this winter and has got quite thin. I wormed her and took her for some blood tests, but there was nothing obviously wrong. Then we worked out that she must be 10 or 12 years old so, I suppose, she's entitled to be thin and tired. She follows me faithfully all day long and this includes when I'm scraping out twice a day.

Mess

As she's long haired (I shear her every year in May), she gets in a bit of a mess. When you have dry weather like we have had in January and March, it dries on her more than usual so when she comes round the corner, she rattles so much it sound like they're doing *Riverdance* in the cubicles.

And me? My wife takes great pride in our highly polished staircase and I came down it much quicker than I expected one morning recently and cracked a bone in my shoulder. And no, I wasn't.

It wasn't quite as bad as the time I fell down the stairs at Bishops Castle Rugby Club one Christmas – which was an ambulance and blue light job – and I managed to milk that morning, but haven't for three weeks since. The moral of the story, put your socks on when you get to the kitchen.

I could write a separate article about this, but some time ago we decided that the viability of our business could no longer depend on the price of leasing quota. We determined not to pay high prices any more and to milk to the quota we had. As a result, our farm has, over the past three months, undergone it's most dramatic changes ever. We have become poultry farmers, one broiler shed up and running and another under construction.

All our resources are going into setting this up, so we will probably only milk 50 cows this year and go back up to 80 next. I'm off to walk round the chicks now, the trouble is I keep forgetting their names, there's 27,000 of them.

June 1997

A few years ago we had a policy of buying semen from good bulls and balancing that with semen (I've just looked out of the window and it's snowing, never mind it'll be nice and warm in the chicken sheds) from young bulls, the aim being to bring down the average price. Describing anything we do as a policy is almost an accolade, but anyway, that's what we used to do.

Cattle breeding being what it is, it will come as no surprise to you to know that for a few years, all the £25 semen produced bull calves and all the £5 semen our heifers. We have two £5 white heifers that are milking at the moment that are a pain in the arse. They are both by the same bull, I won't name him, not wanting to speak ill of the dead (and I certainly hope he is), but unlike all our other cattle they are very flighty.

The sort of thing they do, for example, is when the cows are all standing together in a big lump after milking and you want to get through them to open a gate you have to push your way around each cow because they just stand there ruminating and ignoring you, then you come across one of these heifers and it tries to bolt with such a panic that it frightens all the other cows completely unnecessarily.

As I said last time, for reasons of shiny stairs and gravity I haven't been on full power lately and had missed milking for a month. The first day back, last week, I was milking away and quite enjoying it. Our cows enter our circular abreast parlour through a sort of race and one of these white heifers had been standing there for about ten minutes trying to make her mind up if she recognised me or not, and whether to come in to be milked. It didn't hold up milking because the other cows could get past her and I wasn't bothered if she stayed out till last (I might have a bad shoulder, but there was nothing wrong with my boot or my voice).

I was busy changing a unit when she suddenly let out a fearful roar. The sort of noise a cow will make if you have her in a crush and you are giving her an injection with a needle that you have made out of a hollowed out six-inch nail. Still roaring, she charged across the parlour and leapt into the only empty stall with such force that she ended up in a heap at the front.

She disentangled herself, had another good roar, took a swing at me as I put the chain behind her and then waited to be milked as if nothing had happened. With her and me, there were 15 of us in the parlour and, as far as I know, I was the only one who didn't defecate, but it was a close thing.

When I first came to live here, our AI service came from Knighton, indeed I represented Knighton sub centre on the North Wales committee for a few years. For about 30 years we had the same three inseminators and the four of us have grown old together. Then, Knighton was closed and our service came from Llandrindod Wells, but the inseminators stayed the same, that's the main reason why we have never gone DIY AI, well we've all got to make a living (with a bit of luck).

Llan'dod eventually closed and we were moved to Usk, retirement and ill health brought us a new inseminator, from Brecon, and on we went quite happily. I got to know the people on the phone, I had gossip all the way from Bridgend to Bishops Castle, I could find out what my friends around Cwmbran were up to, all very satisfactory.

Now I hear that Usk is to close and the business moved to Worcester. I sometimes wonder if the new Genus has a sort of death wish. I always thought that there was already a very successful AI company based in Worcestershire. When top management are playing efficiency games on their computers, they never take account of the loyalty that local people feel to other local people that live and work in their locality.

First person in the pub: "Fred is drinking fairish lately, his Land Rover has been outside the pub twice a day for a fortnight now."

Second person: "I saw that, he must have stopped for a quick pint on the way back from the vet, there was a ewe in the back."

Third person: "Fred never takes a ewe to the vet. As soon as he starts lambing he puts a ewe in the back of his Land Rover with a bucket of water and a wad of hay. Every time his missus hears the Land Rover going off the yard, she looks out of the window, sees the ewe and thinks he's off to the vet. He's really off to the pub, it's the same ewe all the time and he leaves her there for about three weeks."

Nothing much new in life. Been going to physiotherapy. First day there's a familiar tub hanging on the treatment table. "This will put you right," I'm told. "I've had plenty of that," I reply. It's just Uddermint with the label scrubbed off.

It's still snowing – off now to find a vest.

July 1997

I suppose that if you go on doing your best for a long period of time, in this case over 30 years, you will, almost inevitably, get something right.

I refer, with a degree of self-satisfaction, to our silage making. Most of us expected to be early this year. It was an early season in most respects, but as the time to cut arrived, the weather did its best to delay things.

We were so lucky to snatch ours in a two-day dry period. We cut on a dry day (14 May) and it was all picked up the next day. In fact the sheet and tyres were on by 7 pm that night.

It was the first time we have ever done it before the West Mid Show, which is usually the criteria for being early around here. After that, the heavens opened and there was little done for about ten days.

In fact, so protracted seemed the wet spell and so few people had done any silage, that I started to feel a little guilty. Not for long mind, guilt is an emotion you can come to terms with and it took me about ten minutes.

We have a workshop, carpenters and other tradesmen have workshops and I thought that was it, but apparently not. Around here, and everywhere else I suspect, we have these new people who also have workshops. In our small village, people I don't know, who I have never heard of, are holding story-telling workshops, drama workshops, painting workshops, the list is endless.

They haven't caught the imagination of the real locals like, for example, the Sunday lunchtime fight at the pub two weeks ago, but you shouldn't mock too much. What all these workshops have in common is an ability to pull money from the lottery and the EU to pay all their expenses.

I wrote one of my letters to the local press to announce farming and rural life workshops to be held in the pub on Saturday nights. So far, we have discussed how the sheep are shearing, how late a friend of ours was with his silage this year, a whole range of topics, including sex and gossip. We haven't had a lottery grant yet but when we do it will go behind the bar to defray expenses.

People keep asking me when I will mention my chickens, well it doesn't really seem appropriate, but when it does, I will. Like all farming it has its disasters. One of the best sights is all those lovely day-old chicks running about on clean shavings in the warm. Then you go back two hours later and a bloody pipe has burst and a quarter of the shed is three inches deep in water and all the chicks are trying to drown themselves.

And finally there's the chicks' nipples. The chicks don't have nipples, they drink out of them and you have to keep them clean. So you fit a filter to the mains water supply. Recently I wrote about excessive chlorine in our water supply. I change the filter every two weeks and you should see the state of it, now I'm glad there's chlorine in it.

August 1997

The old bitch (the dog that is) has a job to move them, so I loose the young one as well (she's out of control). They're OK on the out run, but they could do with the help of a couple of Rottweilers on the fetch. Then they put up a rabbit and the cows are put on hold while they give that a bit of a run.

I was talking about the June weather with my friend Ian Watson from Carlisle, he said: "It's a bit clarty with us as well." What do you reckon that means? I reckon it's Cumbrian for shitty.

September 1997

We were going to reduce our herd to about 50, something to do with cashflow and new chicken sheds, but some of the suppliers to the sheds have been pretty relaxed about finishing their work, so I have been pretty relaxed about paying them. The trade on cows has been erratic so I shan't sell any more and we'll go into the winter at around 70. I tried to sell them at home and quoted an average price. One buyer turned up, picked out the best cow, and wanted to take her at the same money. In his dreams!

Everyone is naturally disappointed about the reduction and ceiling on the value of cull cows at the moment, but my own concern is how much longer will the Government go on paying for disposal? Will cull cows ever go back into the food chain? I certainly hope so, or the day will surely come when we will have to pay for disposal ourselves. It would mean that longevity could be the most important criteria in breeding selection and reconciling longevity with the low cell counts that the consumer apparently demands the most difficult.

The last cows that I sent off were carted all the way up into Lancashire, even though they were booked through a group only about 50 miles away. I was very upset actually as there were a couple of old favourites included that would, in the past, have had a short pleasant journey down to Ludlow. The abattoir in Ludlow is not allowed to participate in the cull. They tell us to improve welfare and then totally disregard it themselves. We live in a world of double standards.

October 1997

When I was at school, we had an English teacher with whom I had a love/hate relationship: she loved to hate me. But, one thing still sticks with me from her lessons: every week we had to learn five new words and use them in our weekly essay. So, as I write now all these years later about welfare issues and so on, the word that comes constantly into my mind is: plethora. It means "glut" in this context. And that's exactly what we have now - a plethora of schemes on welfare, traceability and due diligence.

What I would like to see is all these schemes brought together under a national standard so that we are all together on this. It shouldn't be a competitive issue between farmers, or milk buyers, and there should be no duplication.

We are involved, like it or not, in evolutionary changes in cow welfare and facilities and when we have all this in place, then we should get Government approval for what we have done and what we are doing. Some of you may throw your hands up in horror at Government involvement in this, but we need to have Government backing to fight against double standards.

The supermarkets can take the high moral ground on all these issues, but if someone with no standards at all offers them some product at a penny a pound less, their standards fly out of the window. I really believe that the Government would back us on this.

At the moment (when imports of food are flooding in because of the state of sterling), there is chicken coming in from South America - where they couldn't give a shit about people so God knows what it's like being a chicken - and butter from some country where they mutilate their cows, shoot their calves on the side of the road and play excellent rugby.

Going organic?
There seems to be a chance that we might go organic. It won't be my decision. I shall leave it to David, but he hasn't said much about it lately because he has more serious things

on his mind. He's captain of Ludlow 1st XV again and he has to worry about second-row forwards with sore shoulders, and geriatric centres with bad knees.

We come at it, not as enthusiasts, but as a means of adding value. Having said that, we will go for it wholeheartedly if we do, and won't cut any corners. Our consultant suggested it first. He said: "There are only a very few of my clients who could handle it and, of those, I think you would do it best, because you're more of a crank than the rest of them."

That's the first time he's paid me a compliment. I confess to having a few reservations. If organic farming is at one end of the spectrum and modern high-tech farming at the other, there seems a chance that there will be pressure to step back a bit from the hi-tech to a greener way. If so, the gap between the two would narrow as would the commercial advantages. Organic farming is a niche market. The trick will be to judge how big this niche is.

I was disappointed to find that we will not be allowed to use chicken muck as fertiliser. "We do not want organic farming to be associated with the by-products of factory farming," said the man. You can treat sick animals with antibiotics, but there are huge withdrawal periods. (Antibiotics are either there, or they're not – no grey areas.) If I grow conventional cereal crops on my "away" land, I can't feed the grain, but I can feed the straw.

Whatever, it looks as though I could spend my twilight years as a farmer attacking weeds with either a long-handled hook or a hoe, which is exactly the way I started.

November 1997

When you have two chicken sheds with 28,000 chickens in each shed, it's quite difficult to build up a personal relationship with individual chickens. I was delighted therefore to find a black chick in one shed when our last crop arrived. When I go on my rounds I pick Blackie up (no shortage of imagination here when it comes to naming things) and make a fuss of him.

As I sat in the kitchen on Sunday morning, contemplating

my first cup of tea and my hangover, it occurred to me that I hadn't seen Blackie the day before, neither for that matter, had I seen my dog.

I searched for the dog first, but to no avail. We're usually so close that if I walk across the yard and stop she bumps into me. I went to the chickens next and the dog was in the chicken shed, all very cosy at 29°C while it was raining like hell outside. I soon found Blackie, and picked him up and gave him a cuddle.

I was just about to put him down when another black chick came running up to me. So I had two black chicks all the time. As I said it's not easy building up personal relationships with 28,000 chickens in one shed.

December 1997

All around the country, welfare accreditation, in its various forms, is gathering pace. A lot of farmers are wary of it, suspicious of its need and in its application. It's still a relatively new concept and suspicions are understandable.

We had a sort of open day here last week. I opened the farm up for a Milk Marque assessment and I was pleased with the numbers that turned up. I hope that they found it useful. I just hoped that seeing me being assessed gave them some idea of what to expect when their turn came.

I didn't do anything in preparation, well not on the welfare front, just a bit of tidying up. I keep doing odd things, (that sounds odd in itself), I keep doing small jobs that improve the dairy and parlour and had decided to put a wash basin in the dairy. I ordered it some time ago, but it only appeared the day before the visit. I've painted the dairy out this summer, but the new copper pipes weren't painted – quite a few spotted that. I'd targeted the two days before for most of the tidying up, but things were set back when David broke his finger (rugby), but I don't think things looked too bad. I parked the van in front of the workshop door, which was falling off anyway.

I sometimes get the chance to sit in on the next lot of assessments that are bearing down on us. I know a lot of farmers will baulk at the extra paper work involved. I hope to involve my vet in a lot of it. Our vets have always carried treatments away in their heads.

I am hoping that we can spend a few minutes after each visit logging down treatments and drugs so that my records and the vet's records always tie in accurately together. A bonus will be that the vet's involvement each step of the way will authenticate everything I do, where it is appropriate. His participation in my record keeping will give me back-up when the man from the supermarket eventually turns up.

For many of you, this due diligence and traceability is a nightmare scenario, but there are two important factors you mustn't forget. A food agency was inevitable, regardless of who won the election.

The Government will listen to consumer groups and the supermarkets. If we don't participate it will all happen any way, don't be under any illusions about that, so we might just as well be involved and hopefully have some influence.

Secondly, I can live with all the hassle and the extra paperwork if it stops supermarkets from importing food from countries with no standards at all. That has got to be the eventual aim.

May 1998

I'm supposed to be writing every month again now. Difficult times, they said, cheer everybody up. What I want to know is who's going to cheer me up? It does concern me that, in a supposedly caring society, people get cheered up by reading about the misfortunes of others.

Having just a few cows to milk does you no good at all. I've got the little dictionary on the table that I used in school. Sloth and sluggish are the two most apt words to describe me in recent mornings. My alarm has been going off at 5.30 am. I've been getting up at six – well sixish – having two leisurely cups of tea, milking, scraping up, forking the silage and feeding the young cattle and coming back in by 7.30 am for another cup of tea before going to see the chickens. The alarm clock is half my trouble. It's a conventional one and easily fits the most important criteria for a good alarm clock

117

– you can switch it off without waking up. This is particularly important for me because I have some of my best dreams after the alarm goes (You wouldn't believe what I dreamt this morning).

Over the years, my daughter has bought me cockerel alarms that crowed and said good morning when you switched them off and soldier alarm clocks that blew bugles. They had one common advantage – I hurled abuse at them as I switched them off. This in itself would interrupt dreams and get me up. Now I've got a proper herd to milk, it's easy to get up again.

When I've had another birthday. I told a friend that I had just started another lap, he asked if it would be the last one. Well you never know, do you? Ann reckons I've reached the stage where I have more to remember than I have to look forward to – not if I have anything to do with it.

June 1998

Here we are, nearly half way through the year and nothing has gone right yet. The May issue of *Dairy Farmer* arrived at breakfast time and I announced that I didn't like the new photo they had used. I said it made me look a miserable old bastard. No one said a word.

Then I went for a medical; a health check they call it. It went OK to start with. Blood sugar, pulse and so on, then they put me on the scales. The nurse consulted a chart: "According to this you should be seven feet six inches," she said. Urine next; they compare the colour to a colour chart, the nurse held the chart over the sink to compare colours, "I suppose this will be alright. Most people put their sample in a bottle."

I don't know why, perhaps it was because I'd still got cleanish clothes on, but I went for a haircut in the afternoon. I go to this up-market ladies' hairdressers, it's a bit expensive, but sometimes it's worth it when they keep brushing against you with their boobs.

You usually have to make an appointment, but I remember years ago passing the hairdressers and needing a haircut, so I popped my head through the door. They were very busy, but I asked the lady who owns it if there was any chance of a quickie. "Twenty minutes be all right?" "That'll be fine," I replied, "any chance of a haircut afterwards?"

She went red, but all the customers were very amused. I'd expected to feel a bit cold down the back of my neck afterwards, but I hadn't actually expected snow to lodge on my collar.

Badger discovery

We don't get around our ground much in the winter, no sheep now, but when I did start to get busy I was delighted to find two new badger setts in the middle of the farm. My first reaction was: just when you think things can't get any worse.

Friends and neighbours have plenty of ideas on what to do to move them, but the one sett is under an oak tree in the middle of a field and very conspicuous. I spurned their advice on slurry, diesel and creosote, but I did think I was within my rights to piss down them, the dogs took their cue and did the same.

I must have piss like the Pied Piper because the setts became noticeably bigger afterwards. One of them is on the edge of a field that always hosted a lot of skylarks. They all but disappeared recently, but have made a comeback this year. I bet a foraging badger will soon hoover their nest up.

By coincidence, we had a TB test recently. One heifer had to be retested and now has to be tested again. It's a bit like sitting on a time bomb. I need a positive reactor like I need bad weather, a strengthening pound and TB-infected badgers roaming about my land.

I can see my big Brown Swiss cow on her hands and knees grazing under the wire as far as she can. She tests the system all day, every day and I long for a long-range air rifle to give her a smack up the arse.

She has half a dozen fifth columnists following her up and down hoping for a breakthrough. I don't know what fifth columnists are, but that's what my blacksmith used to call anyone he didn't like.

July 1998

All that glitters is not gold. A friend of mine found that out, working away from home on a very hot day and forgot to take a drink with him. In the end, the sight of the sparkling brook at one end of the field became too much for him and he got down on his belly and had a good lap.

He didn't have to worry about taking a drink anywhere for the next three days because he didn't dare go more than five yards from a toilet. Local legend has it that this river is the only one that runs out of England into Wales. There's got to be a moral in that somewhere.

September 1998

We've been buying sawdust from a local saw mill for the chickens. It's cheaper if you fetch it yourself (compared with buying it in bulk) and as it's fresh, it's damper, and therefore increases the humidity in the sheds for the baby chicks which, apparently, is a good thing.

Anyway, me and the dog go to fetch this sawdust; I park on the weighbridge and go in to get my ticket and the dog goes off for a look round. I go on and get loaded, can't see the dog anywhere, give her a whistle, here she comes out of a shed with somebody's sandwiches.

Decide we'd better move quickly off, so back to the weighbridge, get the ticket stamped and off home. Halfway home and the dog has finished the sandwiches and looking very pleased with herself. I'm not quite so pleased because it has just occurred to me that I have just paid £30/tonne for my own dog and somebody else's lunch. No wonder I'll never be rich.

A friend of mine asked me to go and judge his local farms' competition. I took a friend along with me because we were judging arable farms and I actually know less about arable farming than I do about dairy farming, if that were possible.

I didn't let you down though and I was soon talking very knowledgeably about earwashes and seed numbers per square metre. After a couple of farms I was able to tell the difference between wheat and barley, and even asked the farmers questions.

The big question, however, remained unanswered. I thought about it for several days afterwards. With no stock to care for, what the hell do they do in the winter?

We find ourselves farming in times when every single penny counts. We had these two Limousin calves, a bull and a heifer, that we were due to sell in a few days' time and they were suckling a cow.

They were so fit that it was no easy job to get the cow into the box before they came out and legged it. I had to give them a serious bollocking before I could open the door for the cow, and they would go so fast around the box that I'm pretty sure they did parts of the circuit running on the walls.

I let the cow in yesterday and one calf was dead. Not stretched out, just lying down, perfectly composed, but very dead. I let the cow in and trudged off across the yard. David came around the corner and I said: "One of those bloody calves is dead." He asked if it was the bull or the heifer (We're talking £60 compared with £160 here). "I've been farming long enough now to know that I don't need to look," I replied. And I was right.

October 1998

There were lots of people in the pub one Saturday night a couple of weeks ago. There'd been a wedding in the town and they were having a drink on the way to the after-wedding party (I was invited as well).

They were all having to stand up because the regulars had got all the seats, in fact there was only one empty seat in the place, next to me, which was unusual because there's usually an empty seat either side of me.

The women were all dressed to kill, you know the sort of thing, "look how smart I can look, look at my posh outfit, I should have been invited to the day job not just the evening do."

Anyway they kept chattering away, and looking over their shoulders because you can see that really they would prefer to be sitting down. And I think to myself, "I'm going to get one of them sitting by me in a minute." So I start to run my eye over them, as you do, wondering which one it will be and eventually someone does come and sit by me. A bloody farmer! I actually knew him by sight but couldn't think who he was (he was dressed up a bit as well). Turns out he had spent a day at our place helping the contractor with our first-cut silage. I didn't recognise him because the only other time I'd seen him he was wearing a boiler suit and a Ford tractor. I think he farms corn, beef and sheep.

He leant over, "You're interested in dairy farming." "Just a bit." "Well," he says, "I buy my milk off a milk roundsman, and they've just put the price up to 39p a pint." (We're talking early July here, pre Milk Marque selling round.) "I phoned them up several times to enquire why the price of my milk was going up, they said they'd phone back but they never did."

"Back in the spring I got a pint of milk out of the fridge," he continued. "I like a pint of milk to drink, anyway, but it wouldn't come out of the bottle. I phoned the milkman, he said he'd had a circular from his dairy to say it was due to farmers putting something in the milk. I phoned the dairy, they said the milk wouldn't come out of the bottle because the farmers were giving the cows something to eat that made the milk too creamy to come out of the bottle."

He went on up the trail of dairy hierarchy. "Well, what's happened is the cows were out at grass, the weather went wet, the cows came back indoors, their diet changed and the milk went too creamy." "But you take the cream off the milk." "How do you know that?" "Well I'm a farmer." "Oh we didn't know you were a farmer, we wouldn't have told you that if we'd known you were a farmer."

My friend suggested the possibility that the milk wouldn't come out of the bottle because it was stale. The dairy said they'd get back to him on that and in the meantime they would arrange for him to have a week's free milk. He's had the milk but heard no more.

The moral of this story is that if he had a pint of stale milk, there's a fair chance that others did. If they complained they would have been told it was the farmers' fault. I gave him full marks for persistence on behalf of other farmers, a lesson for us all there.

Bambi

At long last I've got a Brown Swiss heifer calf out of my Jersey cow. I bought her years ago at a neighbour's retirement sale and since then she's had two Brown Swiss bulls, two Jersey bulls and two Limousin heifers. I've always fancied breeding a Brown Swiss out of her because we can mate it pure again, up to nearly pure eventually. At least we have the right colour to start with.

My grandson has named the calf Bambi after one of our favourite videos, which is quite fortunate for the calf - it could easily have been called Gonzo or Miss Piggy.

January 1999

I'll tell you what really pisses me off – Christmas trees. We've been into this Christmas tree farming for years now. We've got only one wood on our farm, it's just a couple of acres, long and narrow, with a power line running down the length of it. Half of it is my sort of conservation area, stream, pond and so on, while the other half we have to keep under some control because of the power line. So we grow Christmas trees on it. A sort of four-year rotation, a quarter of it cleared and planted every year.

There's always something going wrong with them. Last spring my contractor decided to spread my slurry right up to the edge of the adjoining field – to get it nice and thick along the edge, it meant that a 20-yard strip of Christmas trees got it nice and thick as well. "Is that the remains of a bird's nest at the top of my tree Mr Evans?" "No it's cow shit."

The biggest problem is always the sales side. The marketing of these trees seems to attract people from the lower end of life's social scale. People like Will Carling and people who drive around in Transit pick-ups with chrome wheels and call you sir. You throw 300 trees onto a lorry at an agreed £3 apiece and when you've finished they say they will only pay you £2. People who come along in November before you've cut them, order 500 at £4 and you never see them again. These sort of people are never on the phone. We've tried all ways. One year we carted them all to an auction in Worcestershire, the trade crashed and we had to pay to have them removed in a skip.

Some people often tell me that I am a bit "one eyed" with regard to my support for Milk Marque. Everything in life is relative. Ann and I had the chance to go to see Manchester United play at Old Trafford. You've never seen "one eyed" until you go there! A couple of weeks later I spent the night in a full MU bedroom in a farmhouse in Pembrokeshire.

Otter nonsense

David is usually more for reading the paper at breakfast than for joining in the conversation, but the other day he did contribute the information that he had seen an otter cross the road in front of him on his way home from the pub. It would be quite easy to be sceptical about this, given the circumstances, but he does have quite a good track record on this sort of sighting.

When he was about 20, he announced one Sunday morning that on his way home from the rugby club the previous evening he had seen a camel looking over a gate. My immediate reaction was "I bet you did", but when I went down to the club the following Saturday, there in the next field was a camel. It owed its origins to a small local family circus that winters in this area. They used to find winter quarters on local farms where security was not always what it should have been. I always thought that they were given a hard time, especially by what I call newcomers to the area. Your real local would be quite philosophical about meeting a brown bear, a baboon, a camel or a zebra walking up the road, shake his head and determine to be a bit more careful about the mushrooms he was eating or to cut down on his drinking. Your newcomer is more for his petition and his action group.

However, I have no doubt that David did see an otter. It's good news, I've never seen one in the wild and I'm pleased to hear that they are about.

Animals seem to have been quite important in our run-up

to Christmas. My eldest grandson tells me, in all seriousness, that their house is overrun with weasels. For those of you who have never seen the video *Wind in the Willows*, weasels are very low life, like Christmas tree buyers. They emptied his advent calendar of sweets the first night it was put up and they keep using his mother's computer to write letters to Father Christmas.

I expect that by now most of you have spent your share of the £120 million handout. I thought it was quite brilliant, for the Government. Public opinion was on our side, goodness knows what would have happened if the calf scheme had come to an end. For a relatively modest sum, they solved everything overnight. If we continue to complain we will look like a really whingeing lot.

February 1999

The further we go into the year at least the days get longer. We might have a spring, and all these "drinks" and "at homes" seem to die out. I'm not really into midday socialising, either it turns out to be such a good do you have to phone up next day and apologise or you spend your time in somebody's kitchen drinking naff wine and picking at bits and pieces they have bought at Marks and Spencer and tried to make look home-made.

If I am totally honest, and occasionally I am, the real reason I don't enjoy these gatherings anymore is because I haven't got a web site. Whatever that is. That's all they can talk about. I don't even understand the jargon. I shrink into the background and into myself and try to be inconspicuous.

Dinner parties are much more difficult. I only went to one, some old friends of mine, gone very yuppie lately. One of the guests was head of a big computer company or something so you can just imagine what the conversation was like. I just kept my head down and got stuck into more than my fair share of the food and wine. Then the inevitable happened, a lull to draw breath in their conversation and the person sitting next to you feels obliged to talk to you. "Do you surf the net?" "I bloody don't." (I'd had a drop by now.) "Well what do you do?"

Shit! What do I do? All eyes on me now. "I play a big bass drum in a brass band." All eyes even wider now. In for a penny, "and I've never even switched a computer on and I've never even got money out of a hole in a wall."

Help was at hand from one of my oldest and best friends at the other end of the table: "nor me, and I once played the trumpet at a dance in Clee Hill village hall and we were booed off the stage after our first number." "Well how on earth do you get cash?" "I cash a cheque in the pub." "And I cash one at the butcher's," cried my friend triumphantly.

And that put life into its true perspective, seems to me. Any dull bugger can play about with computers, and they apparently do, but carrying a big bass drum up the main street in Bishops Castle or playing a trumpet in Clee Hill village hall, well that's the stuff of legends.

Shooting

Shooting remains a big business around here. It never ceases to amaze me that people will pay up to £25 to shoot at pheasants. They could have a shot at me for that sort of money. I used to be in a couple of small shoots, but I only go now when people are kind enough to invite me. I've got all the proper clothes, but I can't get in them any more.

I was invited out for a day just before Christmas. Very convivial. I went to help my host feed some cattle in the evening, there must have been some reaction to the shooting because I fell down three times in the feeding passage. Rumour has it that when I left the shoot earlier, it took me 20 minutes to get my wellies on.

March 1999

January saw a host of television programmes urging people to diet in the New Year. Very timely, especially for me. I've come to the conclusion either me, or my biggest Brown Swiss cow, will have to go on a diet, because at the moment, it's almost impossible to squeeze in between her and the next cow. The omens for losing weight are not good.

A friend of mine has started producing sausages made from pure Tamworth pigs. There are 9kg in our freezer already. He reckons he doesn't kill the pigs until they are almost too fat to walk, which is a slightly different criteria of fitness and fatness to that used by another friend of mine. He rears bacon pigs for his own use and doesn't kill them until they are too fat to see out of their eyes.

We had some people staying here for B & B recently, one of whom was a vegetarian. He was a great one for coming into the kitchen for a chat in the mornings, I went to answer the phone one day and I'm bloody sure he had my bacon sandwich. It was either him or the dog.

Farming is beset by problems, you all know that without me telling you. The trick is to turn things around to your own advantage. There are a lot of soya milk adverts on the television at the moment. This product could be a serious threat to our industry, but if a news bulletin follows the advert what is the most common word in use in one of the items? Soya. We just have to assume that the public have the intelligence to make the connection.

Insurance scheme

Badgers are an emotive subject, but their increase in numbers can be turned to advantage. If you put a vehicle through a hedge, for whatever reason, what better excuse than saying you swerved to avoid a badger? Very noble, putting your own safety second in order to miss the dear little creature.

Illness

I had to have my photo taken for Milk Marque. The photographer normally specialises in photos of cows and bulls. He had me stood on one of those little mounds for ages. I must have caught cold because I've been suffering from flu for a week now. If you haven't had it yet, it is as bad as they say. I did manage to get a couple of days in the house drinking Lemsips and sulking, and when it comes to sulking I can be the most miserable sod you can possible imagine. I just hope that when you read this, you catch it as well.

April 1999

Our subject today is paranoia. So who's paranoid? Me. What about? My heifers again. I'm beginning to think that they see me as some sort of Victor Meldrew character, to be wound up at every opportunity.

I've got this one heifer. She's been calved about three months and always does everything at a trot or a gallop. She's quite smart (well she was), but a bit short of rear udder and if she fidgets while she's milking the tack will fall off her. She's not just quick on her feet, she's quick with them, so it doesn't do to be standing too close when the cluster drops off.

One day I went to get the cows in for milking and she was in the feeding passage, eating all the best silage and shitting on the rest. So I went to undo the gate to fetch her out and she jumped back over the feed fence, which is obviously how she got in. She tossed her head at me, gave a bit of a smirk, and trotted off after the rest of the herd towards the parlour. I know she trotted off after them because I could follow the trail of blood and milk. (I didn't get where I am today without knowing that I've probably just swapped a good heifer for one with three quarters.) One back teat was half off, but we always do our best.

We took her across the yard into a clean pen. The vet knocked her out, put a canula in and tried to stitch the teat back around it. We left her there for the night and I remember thinking I'd leave her there in the morning and the boy could milk her the next afternoon.

I was milking away next morning and into the parlour she came, at about the same time as usual. I thought that the boy had slipped her into the collecting yard for me to milk. I also thought about the quick feet. Anyway, I managed to milk her on three teats and the milk ran out of the canula on the damaged one. At breakfast I said to the boy: "How come I was chosen to milk that heifer first?" Not guilty. Turns out she'd jumped over the gate of her pen, and a fence and two more gates, to get back with the milkers.

We've pushed the yields up in March and I bought a blend for midday feeding. I tried to get some cannabis added to it to calm all these heifers down. At the moment it's as if they see me coming into the yard and say to each other: "Here he comes. Everyone back into a cubicle and shit on the bed." If they were on cannabis they'd say: "Coming to milk us again? Hey, that's really cool."

I'm not against organic farming. In fact we seriously considered it. We had a free advisory visit, but eventually decided against it. One of the reasons was that we weren't allowed to use our poultry manure. "We do not wish to be associated with the by-products of factory farming," said the man, which irritated me a bit. Especially as he said it was OK to put it on our cereal land (which wouldn't be converted) and to use the straw at home. It's the Soil Association that's starting to wind me up. Paranoia again? A few months ago, some of the additives used in pig and poultry feeds were banned. There was a real danger of being knocked over by the Soil Association as it rushed to take the high moral ground. Now it is at it again: "No need to cull badgers on organic farms. TB is not a problem on organic farms."

This statement raises an important question: what is it about organic farms that makes badgers avoid them? Anyone who sets farmer against farmer will see only one loser: another farmer. Don't we have enough against us without turning on ourselves? The real reason that I didn't go organic is its vulnerability to fraud. You can see the idea, you can supply the products and establish the market – at a premium. But what you cannot do is stop some Frenchman taking a kilo of butter or cheese and ripping off the label which tells you it is conventionally produced. They could then replace it with one that tells you that the food is organic and export it here, undermining the premium market you have established.

I always give the milk out of the filter to the cats and dogs. I'm not a cat person and there were 26 of them queued up outside the dairy yesterday morning. I thought that was bad enough, but there were 27 this morning – there was a big ginger tom poking about the yard. I hadn't seen him before, and when I say poking about the yard, the emphasis is on the word poking.

May 1999

As I wend my way through life, farmers' wives frequently tell me that they always read my column – for reasons that completely elude me, they often say that they read it in the toilet. Which brings me quite nicely to my next story, which is definitely indelicate and not really suitable reading for ladies.

One of the problems of the poultry industry (as a consequence of being a chicken farmer) is cheap imports from places like Thailand. A friend of mine knows someone who went to Thailand to see how chickens were produced (this story is only secondhand so it's got to be true) and he came across this unit where the chickens were fed on human sewage. (I didn't go into the technicalities of how they fed it.)

The chicken sheds had wire floors and were built over lagoons, and the lagoons were full of fish which lived on the chicken muck. The chickens and the fish ended up here. I'm not sure in my own mind whether I'd prefer to eat the chickens, or the fish.

If the last story was unsuitable for ladies, this one could be. Last Sunday I went to quite an important rugby match at Wembley. You may have seen reports of it, or even watched it on television. At half-time I went for a pee (as you do when you get to my age). The crush in and around the toilets was unbelievable.

As I was standing there, peeing, I became aware of someone pressing up very close behind me. Not feeling very comfortable, but unable to do anything about it, I looked over my shoulder and discovered a huge bouncer-type. I was somewhat relieved to find that his undivided attention was on the person peeing to my left, as was the attention of two other big men who were obviously with him. Naturally I turned my interest to the person next to me. It was Tom Jones. Yes, The Tom Jones. Well you have to look don't you?

It was about the same size as mine, but hadn't got as much rust on it. I have to ask you, in all seriousness what other farming journal, other than *Dairy Farmer*, could bring you information like that?

June 1999

My wife is seriously into gardening. Just outside our back door she invariably has a bag of garden compost and her flower pots. There's these two little boys who come to our place on a regular basis - they reckon I'm their granddad. For a couple of years now they have been playing with this compost, putting it in tiny tractors and trailers and moving it between flower beds – no mess, no damage, no hassle, good as gold. Suddenly, one Saturday morning, the game changed. Pedal tractors and trailers appeared. Suddenly we were into serious muckspreading. In half an hour our back yard looked as though it had been targeted by a NATO bombing raid. I was chosen to divert them to something else. I have never been a carpenter - I'm more your six-inch nail, hammer and chainsaw carpenter - but I did manage to convert a fairly large cable reel into a reasonable copy of a tractor roller. I sent the oldest boy off to roll the lawn feeling quite pleased with myself. He went round the lawn once and came back to ask why he hadn't got a gang of three rolls that folded up hydraulically like his Uncle Rob has got.

Exchange rate
There is not much sign of things getting better financially. Every evening I put the exchange rates up on Ceefax and most of the changes are in the second decimals. There are plenty of stories about just how tight money is on farms. There was a local store-cattle show and sale last week and they asked the bank manager to present the cup. He walked into the market at one end and about 20 farmers were badly trampled in the rush to get out at the other.

July 1999

Cattle behaviour
"The effect of spring grass on cow behaviour" sounds a bit pretentious and like the title of a thesis for my PhD. What we'll probably get is something of a standard more akin to a school essay.

For years now, I have been fascinated by the changes that occur in some cows' behaviour, usually in May, when they are getting as much lush spring grass as they can possibly eat. The change usually manifests itself as one for the worse. Nervousness where it didn't exist, bad temper where once there was none, and even refusing to let milk down. And it isn't always the same cows.

This year, like most, it is noticeable in two or three. Take, for instance, just one of our cows. Most of the milking year she's called Sweetie. For the past three weeks she's been called Bitch, usually preceded by an adjective and usually the same one.

The change in her behaviour this year has been dramatic. Most of her milking year, she is in the first 14 that come into our parlour. Being in the first 14 means that she is highly competitive. I used to think that this initial rush was something to do with my own charisma, but apparently it's because we feed cake in the parlour. If a cow is consistently among the first in the parlour, it's because she's aggressive towards her contemporaries, she's probably greedy, and, to a lesser extent, she doesn't mind being milked.

Number 103 fitted into this scenario quite neatly. Or she did until the herd went out to grass. Now she comes in last. You have to fetch her in most milking times, she is usually in the furthest corner of the collecting yard with her arse towards you and her head down as if she's found a pound coin on the floor and she's trying to find a way to pick it up. Sometimes she lashes out at you as you turn her towards the parlour. Anyone would think you were trying to drive her into an abattoir.

Even when you get her in to milk, she doesn't always let her milk down. But that's not the whole story – not by a long way. Remember I said she was aggressive? She spends the whole milking time stopping other cows going into the parlour as well.

You run out of cows and go out into the yard and she's got them all backed up at the far end. Nothing can get past her, she moves back and forth like a well-trained sheep dog. Correctly channelled, this habit could see us both on television – one man and his cow.

I mentioned this phenomena in *Dairy Farmer* years ago and someone phoned to say they thought it might be due to too much protein. I don't know why it happens, but then I'm quite thick. I do know that a month from now she'll be called Sweetie again.

Meanwhile, life on the farm goes on. You have your bad days and sometimes you have your good ones. I found my penknife in a field of oats. I got a live bull calf and didn't do any damage (after a difficult calving) to a heifer that had had under-age sex with a neighbour's Simmental bull. (We had intended to induce her a week early, but it's not that easy when you didn't witness the illicit liaison).

I went for petrol in the farm van. My friend at the garage said, without any enthusiasm: "I reckon that van's about due for its MOT. I've failed plenty of vans for going rusty, but this will be the first one for going mouldy."

I wasn't going to tell you this next bit, but I will because I'm so excited. Some of the best friends I've made in life and some of the best fun I've had have been because of rugby. The best fun of all has been going with those friends on trips. You start off with rugby tours, our first one was at Easter on the Isle of Wight 30 years ago and we still talk about it. As you get older, you will go on trips with the friends and the fun is just as good, but you don't have to play rugby.

Well, one of these good friends is 60 this year and, to celebrate, he's paying for me and another friend (when I say he is paying you will know we are not talking about a farmer here) to go to South Africa, Zimbabwe and Mauritius. Two weeks of good fun and a safari.

I told them I didn't want to go anywhere near to crocodiles or snakes. No problem, they said, adding that the dusky maidens are far more dangerous. My grandsons think I'm bringing them back a lion cub and a jumbo.

I'm not too sure about white-water rafting on the Zambezi. Do they have toilets on the rafts? We finish up with four nights on Mauritius in a luxury hotel. Life can be a bitch sometimes, but you have to make the best of it.

August 1999

My mood this week has been philosophical. Yesterday, during the morning milking, I was putting the chain behind the first cow in the parlour – probably not as alert as I should have been – and she pissed down my welly. I took the act philosophically. I didn't retaliate, but carried on as if nothing had happened. Having a cow piss down your welly is a bit like an MMC inquiry report. Half an hour later, I decided it was also a bit like life – quite pleasant to start with, all warm and moist, but now it was uncomfortable, squelchy and cold.

I've done the first-cut thistle harvest, but I'm fairly confident that we'll have a second cut. We've bought a secondhand topper which is just as well as I've broken the hook I use round the outsides. I was quite well up with the hand cutting. I follow the cows around so there's not any grass around the thistles. You can do some good daydreaming when you are cutting thistles – I just try not to think about the fact that I was probably cutting the same thistle 35 years ago and have cut it every year since.

I love listening to the sheep farmers chatting in the pub on Saturday nights. They all reckon that they love sheep, but if they do, why is the word sheep always preceded by the "F" word? We're at the time of the year when lamb prices fall every week and they've all just finished shearing. Wool comes in for a lot of abuse as well. The consensus is that they should all dig holes and bury it, but they still haven't worked out how to get it off the sheep without a lot of work and expense. But they're not despondent for long and soon move on to discuss who's got the best dog. One has a dog that will get all the sheep on the farm into the yard while he's having his breakfast. Another has a dog that can do that and bring the cows and calves in too. The best dog, apparently, is the one who brings the ewes, lambs, cows, calves and all the rabbits. The better off among them are the farmers who have good farms, but get £30/ewe hill subsidy. The thinking is that they should keep even more ewes, but not breed them, just draw the subsidy.

Holiday adventure

Now for a long-awaited tale from Africa. We got to our safari camp about midday, had something to eat and set off to look for game – just the three of us and two guides. We'd only gone about 50 yards from the camp when we saw an elephant's arse sticking out from some bushes. We parked the truck and crept up on him until we were only about 15 yards away, but he still didn't know we were there. We watched him for about ten minutes while he carried on browsing in the bushes – when an elephant browses it's very much as a bulldozer grazes a field when there's a motorway under construction.

The elephant worked his destructive way through the bushes until his head popped out about ten yards away and he caught our scent. Up went his trunk and ears, which apparently is elephant speak for I'm not very happy, and the guide said: "If he charges at us, stand your ground." I weighed up the situation and decided bollocks to that – if he charges, I'm off.

The elephant made a bit of a dummy run at us, about three or four steps, but changed his mind and wandered off. The guide said: "Well done, you all stood your ground." I tell him that if the elephant had taken one more step, I'd have made a run for the truck. "If you had run, he'd have chased you and ignored us," replied the guide. That's what he thought, but I'd already worked out that I could keep the guide between me and the elephant at all times – that was part of my plan.

September 1999

I am actually quite enjoying being a dairy farmer at the moment. The farming bit seems to be going OK, it's just the price of milk that is crap. We've got the cows up to about 100 again which is where we were in our pre-chicken days. I haven't told you this before, but I sold some quota to put money into the chicken sheds and now I have to lease so much in, it doesn't do to think about it. Every night I look at Ceefax on page 249 to see the leasing prices.

I am quite pleased with myself and the way I have managed the grazing this year. The layout isn't very handy, but I manage to give the cows fresh grass every evening. I don't bother with back fencing on the biggest paddock - it would be just too complicated with an unfenced council road running through the middle.

We don't have anything as handy as a quad bike here, so I always challenge myself to carry all the fencing kit from one field to the next, in one go. But not in very hot weather. One day, with no shirt on and a pile of plastic fence posts in one arm, I got my nipple trapped between the posts.

I never knew what my nipples were meant for anyway - it's not as if God ever intended me to have a baby.

Goodbye, old friend

Six years ago, I bought a fourth calver Jersey cow at a neighbour's sale. She became a bit of a family favourite. Gertrude was her name and last year she had a smart Brown Swiss heifer calf called Bambi. We couldn't get the Jersey in calf this year so she had to go. I told my haulier to take her next time he had a load of other Jerseys going, I didn't want her knocked about by some big cows. He came one day while I was still milking so I told him he'd have to wait. (The bloody milk tanker comes at 7.10 am). By the time I'd gone in the dairy to put the pipeline to wash, he'd sorted her out, she'd stood still for him to get her ear number and now she was looking at me out of a flap in the lorry with her big brown eyes as if to say: "What have I done to upset you?" I was actually quite upset to see her go.

I felt like a real bastard, but I got over it, as you do, until the following Sunday. "Where's Gertrude gone, Pop?" said my eldest grandson. "She's gone to heaven." He usually accepts deaths if you say things have gone to heaven. "Who will look after Bambi now - mummies are supposed to look after you aren't they?" "She's looking down from heaven to see if Bambi is alright, but I will look after Bambi now." Not convinced, a lot of questioning followed. He's still a bit sceptical that you can get to heaven in a C-reg Scania.

November 1999

Smack in the middle of one of our grazing fields is a dead badger. I haven't been within 20 yards of it. It's nothing to do with me – I don't know how it died or how it got there.

What I have noticed, however, is that if you are a dog, a dead badger is an excellent thing to have a roll on. I haven't had a roll on it myself ,because the other thing I have noticed, is that if you do roll on it, you don't get into the kitchen for three days.

My achievements in life continue to go to greater and greater heights. Just as I seem to think that I have reached some new pinnacle, a whole new experience just opens out in front of me. The latest was to march with the band through Llandrindod Wells on a Sunday morning in the pouring rain. "Boy," I thought to myself, "you've really arrived now."

There's a grocer in our band and we're always winding him up about his goods being past their sell-by date. One of the bandsmen reckons he bought a tin of corned beef there a couple of weeks ago and there was a note inside it that said: "Good luck to our lads on the Somme".

Our road, as we call it, which goes about four miles from a crossroads at one end, to the crossroads at the other, has seen a lot of changes since I came to live here more than 30 years ago. At the breakfast table the other day, we added up how many men were working on the nine farms along the road: there's about 29 men gone in 30-odd years. That's a lot of people when you think about the families as well.

I've decided that I'm not going to shoot anything, so I did wonder just what to do with this fine calf I had. I was pleasantly surprised. Do you remember how I told you that I had swopped some chicken muck for some barley straw? Well, I swopped the Jersey bull. Swopping is a form of barter. Barter is what they had before they had money. Barter is also what some of the "good life" newcomers try to organise around here from time to time. You get these earnest-looking types with a scruffy beard, a baggy pullover, three acres of land and a scruffy goat who, because they've just swopped (or bartered) some cabbage with holes in the leaves for some potatoes with grubs in, think they have saved the world.

Anyway, back to the Jersey bull. The man who takes all my calves has interests in butchery and he has promised me a bag of sausages in return for the calf. This raises two important questions, how many sausages is a Jersey calf worth and are there other Jersey calves in the sausages? Well, you have to ask these questions, don't you? Especially the last one. I know of one dairy farmer in Montgomeryshire who has stopped going to the Indian restaurant.

I went to the Dairy Event for two days, a lot of people came up and said how important it is to keep laughing, so here's a story to finish with.

An auctioneer (the one who sold the Jerseys) was telling me how bad the livestock trade was in general. We ended up discussing the sheep trade and cull ewes in particular.

"Cull ewes are so bad," he said, "that even the people who never pay for them have stopped buying."

December 1999

The other day I was looking at our NFU journal which included photos of members demonstrating at the Labour party conference. Without exception, every farmer was wearing a smile. This isn't how you do it.

Have you ever seen a photograph of the Jarrow march with smiling marchers? What you do is look bloody miserable. I see a career opportunity here: people are always saying to me that I look miserable. It doesn't come naturally, you have to work at it. I could give people lessons.

The Noughties

January 2000

My first constitutional of the new millennium finds me in reflective mood. I've got a hole in my right welly. It's particularly annoying as I've only had the wellies for about six weeks. It says a lot about the profitability of dairy farming that I have tried to mend the hole three times with Superglue. Sometimes I go around with a plastic shopping bag on one foot, sometimes I fôrget. I have to ask myself: should someone in my position – even if I am on my financial arse – be going around with either a wet foot or a plastic bag over his boot?

I've been leasing quota lately and I've still got some more to do. It has taken all my spare money. Am I mad? Are we all mad? Should I be making a note of the names and addresses of the leasors so I can send them a Christmas card and a thank-you note? As I make my way up the yard at 5 am on cold wet mornings, with a heavy heart and slow step (and one of the steps is probably wet), I often ask myself that, if I've paid 8ppl to lease the milk I am just about to produce, is it worth it? Actually you shouldn't ask yourself questions like that because you won't like the answer. The reality is that if you take 8ppl off the price of milk ex-farm, you end up with bugger all.

A couple of years ago we seemed to acquire a black and white bull calf. He was born just at the time of the BSE crisis and was too old to go on the calf scheme. So we reared him. He wasn't a barley beef bull because we don't grow any barley, he was a sort of stock-feed potatoes, silage, dairy cake, antibiotic milk and lawn cuttings sort of a bull. We called him Billy bull – there's never been any shortage of imagination around here. When he was about 14 months old and nearly ready to sell – we were going to put him in the freezer, but we needed the money more – we decided, as part of the very high welfare standards we practise here, to let him have a little bit. Actually he had a little bit three times before he made his way along life's bovine road to the abattoir.

Fair enough, I hope he died with some happy memories, but we've ended up with three heifers by him that are going to the bull at the moment. I don't know, obviously, how they'll milk, but I do know that so far they are minus for type – smart they are not.

Some of my reflections are related to the changes I see in the area where I live. Three or four years ago I was listening to Radio 4 on the tractor and someone said that there were only two tranquil areas left in England. I can't remember where the other one was, but this quiet corner of south-west Shropshire, where I live, was the other. I remember thinking at the time: "I bet that's buggered that." It has and it did. People have flocked here to live, mostly to retire, and their impact is everywhere to see. Nowhere is this more obvious than on the main street of our small local market town. To be fair, a few years ago there were a few empty shops – traditional businesses that were unsustainable as people's shopping habits changed. But these shops are being taken by newcomers and if it's antiques you want, or wish to enhance a trendy lifestyle, look no further. The latest shop is call an "awareness shop – a spiritual store for seekers". What do you reckon they sell in there? I asked a friend of mine the other day: "It's all earth, wind and fire," she said. I temporarily enhance my awareness in the pub every Saturday night, so I can't see me ever going in there.

It's all such a big change from when it was a country town occupied by country people. The local vet used to have a large house on the main street that she used as a surgery. In the spring, farmers would park their Land Rovers out on the street and the vet would come out and lamb ewes in the back of them. Now that was a proper rural scene.

It was interesting for passers-by, it was nice for children who were passing to see lambs being born, and it was part of that scene to see blood running down the gutter. Though to be fair, if it was a market day and there were a lot of people about, they would sluice a bucket of soapy water down the gutter to wash it away when they'd finished.

I've told you before that I grow Christmas trees. I hate them. Two years ago we had about 600 that were of poor quality that we couldn't sell. We left them. This year they were still of poor quality, but about 12 feet long. Suddenly we had an order for 550. We had to get them out quickly last Saturday. The weather alternated between rain, sleet and snow all driven by gale force winds. We had to drag them out of the wood, throw them over a fence, then throw them on trailers. I've never been so cold and wet, but we did it.

Then the buyer phoned to say he'd written his lorry off on the way and couldn't come. Next day he didn't want them. Boy, will we have a millennium bonfire ...

My daughter works in a hospital. On the Monday morning, a colleague asked what she'd been doing over the weekend. "Pulling cold, wet Christmas trees out of a bloody wood."

"Oh, we get ours from Asda," replied the colleague. Sounds alright to me.

February 2000

I decided years ago, that I'm not really a winter person. I've decided that I'm a spring, summer and autumn person. I wasn't ready for this winter and I don't ever recall being ready for any. I wasn't meant to get up when it was dark and go out on damp, cold mornings milking cows. I was meant to spend my winters on a tropical beach, leching at passers-by through my sunglasses. Once a fortnight, I would be whisked away by private jet, in suitably warm clothing, to international rugby matches.

I should never have had to milk cows (I was going to say for a living, but that would hardly be true).

I was lucky enough to have been born perfect in every way. A lot of people couldn't handle something like that, but I've got used to it. However, there is just one modification I would make – I would have fitted grease nipples to my joints. At the moment, I'm having to put Uddermint on my knees every morning just to get up the yard. But there is a glimmer of light at the end of my winter tunnel. Sometime ago I was elected as a farmer director of Axis Milk, one of the new farmer co-ops. It's a whole new experience for me: getting up and putting a suit on, instead of a pair of overalls; getting into the car, instead of a scraper tractor. There are plenty of similarities to dairy farming – long hours and plenty of work.

It's a big task and a big responsibility, one that I undertake with as much commitment and enthusiasm as anything I have ever done. One of the biggest pluses is that the rain is outside and I'm not in it.

We've got a new tanker driver. I'm preparing him for possible bad weather by giving him a cup of tea every morning. I work on the principle that he would try harder to get here if he thought he would get a cup of tea. I hadn't counted on him wanting two spoonfuls of sugar; this is an added expense I could well do without.

I'm not one to point a finger at anyone, but we were two weeks late cutting our wholecrop oats last year and it wasn't my fault. It wasn't down to the weather either. It so happens that a lot of grains are going straight through the cows, with the result that our winter housing is full of cattle, starlings and pheasants. There are more pheasants in the yard most days and I am seriously thinking of letting the shooting, just in the yard. There would be four good drives: the collecting-yard drive, the feed-passage drive, and, best of all, the silage-pit drive.

Suits you, sir
Ann bought me a new suit for Christmas in the January sales. The suit I usually wear seems to have become tight. I hate throwing things away, so a look through my wardrobe is a bit like counting the rings in a tree trunk. The older I get ,the bigger the rings. If I included my new suit and lost a stone in weight, I would have three suits I could wear.

If I lost two stone, I would have five suits. If I lost three stone, I could add another two suits to my wardrobe. These last two suits would have flared trousers. My successful battle against the ravages of anorexia continues.

March 2000

Inspection
We had one of those visits the other day where they want to see your passports and your movements records. They wanted to do it there and then, when they arrived, but we

managed to put it off for a day. It wasn't that everything wasn't in order, but you do have a few jobs of your own to do as well. I thought that I would have to fall back on the old "my son is too busy and I can't read and write" excuse, but it wasn't necessary.

So back they came next day (two of them) and they were here for about five hours. And lo and behold, everything was in order (or very nearly). David had a medium bollocking because some of the ear numbers on the passports were wrong. Not that he had written them down wrong, but they had come back from the Ministry wrong and he should have noticed. There are times in life when it is just as well to say nothing and this was one of them. Unfortunately, those times seem to be increasing.

Anyway, we haven't come to the best bit yet. Most of their time was spent in the house, at midday, so Ann duly offered them some sandwiches and tea – as you do when you want to keep on the right side of things. Quick as a flash – never mind a "yes please" or a "no thank you" – they announced that they were vegetarians. I don't know whether you've noticed, but most vegetarians are anti-livestock farming. Most of them have a hidden agenda to convert everyone they meet to be vegetarian as well. If they are successful, it follows that livestock farming will finish. In the meantime, what better way to play a role in that great crusade, than to work for MAFF and to go around farms inspecting passports? Can you see them being supportive? The trouble is, the buggers are getting everywhere, like a latter-day biblical plague.

We have this thing around here called the Shropshire Hills Countryside Unit. It has money to give away to worthwhile enterprises. Apparently its staff is overrun with vegetarians. What chance is there of me getting some money to start a veal unit for unwanted black and white bull calves? I bet if I wanted to train people to run around waving an oak branch and with a daffodil stuck up their bum, they'd pay for it.

If you really want to know what the enemy is up to, you should try to watch the BBC's *Countryfile* programme on Sunday mornings. The main presenter is a man who became too old to tell the news to children, but who spotted a career opportunity in the "green, environmental, let's blame the farmers industry".

It was a cracker of a programme a couple of weeks ago. It reported on declining water vole numbers on a wetland that had been created near a sewage works. "And what has caused this decline in numbers?" asked the reporter. Here we go, I thought, bet I know the answer to this one. And I did: pesticides and herbicides.

When someone mentions herbicides and pesticides they are blaming the farmer. They are blaming you and they are blaming me. They are pointing a great big finger at you – and it's not the sort of golden finger that comes out and says you have won the lottery. It's the sort of finger that comes out and gives you a sharp prod in the chest, and that can start a fight. But we haven't quite finished yet. *Countryfile*'s naivety is about to reach new heights. At dusk, we are told, this particular wetland is one of the best places anywhere around to watch owls hunting. I know that I'm a bit out of touch on a lot of things, but I don't actually recollect hearing news of a new species of vegetarian owl. In fact, if my memory serves me correctly, owls are quite fond of a bit of freshwater vole. Providing, of course, that your owl can catch one that hasn't already been caught by your mink (also found in wetlands).

Fair play, they did have a recent feature about cull cows having to travel long distances on the scheme, which is something that really annoys me, our cows have to go over 100 miles now where they used to go 14, but the feature didn't have the drive and impact that water voles seem to get.

May 2000

Today I'm assuming the proud mantle of smart arse. I was determined to have the cows out at grass earlier than last year (18 March), and I did. This year it was 11 March. This was a particularly good day for turning out as there was a big farm sale not far from here and a lot of farmers from Montgomeryshire would have driven past.

You are very lucky that this correspondent is at the cutting edge of modern grazing techniques. After they'd been out for two days, I put them out at night as well and they've been out ever since. They have the option to come home for silage and cubicles at all times and most mornings when I go out to milk that's where they are.

We have snow forecast for tonight so they'll be inside. The important lesson for me has been to take advantage of the weather conditions if you can. Not to fix a date for turnout in your mind if nature gives you a bonus – take it. When margins are tight, even non-existent, don't ignore anything that's free.

People have even been asking me about grassland management, which just goes to show what desperate times we live in. They always ask if I have a plate meter. No, I still use the same system I have used for years, though I have refined it a bit lately – up to a crow's shoulders, out at day; up to a corgi's arse, out day and night; wet knees above your wellies, start to cut the cake back. This system has served me well.

My vet seems to have reconciled himself to our paths crossing socially. I suspect I might have embarrassed him occasionally in the past. He seems to have decided to try to make the best of it and to that end is trying to drag me, kicking and screaming, up the social scale.

Last time we went to a rugby match, he decided to teach me about red wine. "The first thing to remember about red wine," he says, "is not to drink too much." I had already worked this out for myself many years ago. So I am scrutinising my vet bills more closely than usual to see if he charges me for this advice.

Bad sheep day

A friend of mine had a bad sheep day last week. He had the lot – difficult lambings, a prolapse or two, sheep out, dead lambs, lambs that wouldn't suck, ewes that wouldn't suckle. Then, last job of the day, move some ewes and lambs on the road. He's training up a young dog and for safety, he tied it to the quad bike to run alongside.

Anyway, along comes a car, pushes through the sheep without much consideration. He succeeds in turning one sheep and her lamb back down the road. He keeps on following the ewe and lamb, driving them even further away.

So my friend has no alternative but to give chase with his quad bike, with dog attached, to fetch the ewe and lamb.

He succeeded. But he was stopped by the driver who gave him a severe bollocking. He turned out to be a plain-clothes policeman. "If I told the RSPCA that you had that dog tied to a quad bike they'd stop you keeping animals for the rest of your life," he said. My friend's reply completely threw him: "Oh, if only they would."

I have a habit and I'm told it's a bad habit. I turn my kitchen chair around and put my feet up on the Rayburn. I find this a comfortable position to read whatever is to hand on the table. The position of my legs, between chair and cooker is also useful.

Two generations of my family have slept there as babies and as they grow older it becomes a bridge – under which live goblins, trolls, dragons and crocodiles.

The two little boys that play there at the moment perform daring rescues in their favoured roles of Tarzan and George of the Jungle. It's not easy being a grandfather these days, you have to compete, trawling your imagination, with Walt Disney. I am winning at the moment, but only just, probably because I'm a better liar than Walt Disney. As the children get bigger and their activities on the bridge become more robust, a succession of kitchen chairs have proved not to be good bridge-building material with the result that half the chairs around our kitchen table are unsafe to sit on.

On Father's Day I was presented with a huge new chair, so big and strong you could use it to build a bridge over a motorway. I'm not allowed to use it yet. The family are going to paint it gold and fit it with a purple cushion. And not before time.

June 2000

One man and his quad
Just lately I have been taking a look, just a sneaky look, at secondhand quad bike adverts. My grandsons have been telling me we really need one for some time now. I made the mistake of taking them for a ride on my son-in-law's. I had the two of

them sitting in front of me. It was a good job they couldn't reach the pedals – four little hands were busy on the controls.

We're at the time of year when I spend a lot of time moving electric fences. One thing is for sure, if there is any milk in docks and nettles, we'll need a new milk tank before long. We practised some extended grazing last year and there's a fair chance I could break an ankle on the rough ground before the summer's over. It's obvious that if you try to turn out earlier and graze later, your land will need a good roll now and again. (Don't we all?)

We're also at the time of year when we have more cows going through the parlour than it was really designed for, so milking is becoming a protracted affair. Some of the magic of fetching the cows on early spring mornings has been lost in the need to fetch them fairly quickly. My old dog is 14 now. She was brilliant at fetching the cows. Some mornings she'd already be down the fields, perhaps lying quietly under a tree, never disturbing the cows until she heard your first call. By the time you had the parlour ready she'd have the cows well on their way home. These days she just stands in the yard and barks encouragement. Now we have her daughter. After suitable verbal abuse, she goes at high speed out around the cows, who may be half a mile away. On a television programme for sheep dogs she would score 19 out of 20 for her outrun. The trouble is she doesn't do anything when she gets there, so she would probably be -10 for the lift.

So we have up to 120 cows lying down chewing the cud on a lovely spring morning about half a mile away with this young dog standing next to them. As I stumble along the cow track, my calls become more animated and one of the Jerseys leaps to her feet and sets off towards home at a purposeful trot.

Half the cows decide they could be missing out on something here, get to their feet, stretch, empty their bowels in huge heaps exactly where they plan to be lying tomorrow morning, and set off home after the Jersey cow at reasonable speed. This is good. Now one of the other Jerseys gets to her feet, she empties herself out at her leisure, has a good stretch and charges after the dog. As a spectator sport for cows, this is apparently excellent. The rest of the cows get to their feet and follow closely in order to watch. As the dog has performed so well on her outrun she is inevitably on the far side of the cows and, just as inevitably, she gets chased the wrong way.

So I end up with half the cows coming home and the other half going away. This is not so good. The dilemma is, should I train the dog to go first as far as the first cow she comes to, so that they all chase her home, or should I have another look at those quad bike adverts?

We took a field of grass keep, 21 acres, in the village. It was a bit of an impulse buy really but my thinking was that if you have half your annual rainfall in April then it's bound to be a dry summer. I can live with January weather in January, but I don't like it in April. The field wasn't very expensive because it's in the stewardship scheme and I can only put 13 heifers there until the end of June. It's low-lying land so it could keep a lot of dry cows in late summer if keep gets tight at home. In fact the field is only 200 yards from the pub so it will probably cost more to go to see the cattle every day then it did to rent the field.

A friend of mine goes on these Farmers for Action demonstrations. So his wife says: "How come you'll spend every night standing outside Sainsbury's, but you won't come with me in the daytime?"

I went on a four-hour train journey earlier this week. I farmed it all the way there and back. I couldn't believe the low numbers of livestock. If ever there's a famine in this country, we'll all be eating horses.

July 2000

Home Truths

"Why don't you just tell them to —— off?" The questioner was at the back of the room at a meeting I attended in Cardiganshire last winter. The word I've left blank is one I've heard only a few times, so I'm not sure how to spell it. He was referring to Farm Assurance and there was a lot of sympathy for his views in the room.

The main things in life are fairly simple, it is usually the detail that becomes complicated. It is a simple basic fact of life that if you tell a customer to do what my first line tells them to do, before very long you will lose that customer.

If your wife sells eggs at the door and they are white eggs and your customers say the eggs are fine, very tasty, with nice rich yellow yolks, BUT, they would really prefer brown eggs. Unless you go to Hereford market one Wednesday and buy some point-of-lay pullets which lay brown eggs, pretty soon you won't have any customers. Farm Assurance is as simple as that. It is annoying, because it comes riding on the back of BSE. I have a theory, that in time, farmers will not get the blame for BSE. I also suspect that farmers of my age will never know the truth about BSE.

The truth will open a can of worms that could bring governments down. So it may not emerge for another 30 years, when it surfaces in some cabinet papers. (I'll probably have to wait until one of you younger ones dies and comes up to tell me.)

There are some pluses to Farm Assurance. First, it's apparently nowhere near as bad as you think - failures are usually down to minor detail, locks on dairy doors and medicine cupboards, stuff like that. Second, the supermarkets are starting to inspect farms on the Continent, at long last. Because, deep down it's double standards that irritate most.

It will be interesting to see if the controversial adverts in the press at the moment make any impact on retail sales of pig meat. I watch those glossy Jersey cows grazing their green (virtual reality) landscape on the television, and I think 'just you wait'. I think Farm Assurance is something we can all take in our stride; everyone keeps telling us we are part of a global market, let's take the lead.

The weather has been pissing me about lately. It's June 5 today and I haven't done my first cut silage yet. It's June 5 today and already, we've had 50mm of rain this month. The wet April meant we put our barley and peas in nearly a month late, then all the pigeons and crows in the parish tried to eat them.

There are still lots of wonderful things in life – memorable rugby matches, sunny spring mornings, little children and miniskirts. Right up there is chicken muck. From trial and error, we have found that the best time to give this farm a good dosing is in January (preferably in a frost). December or February will do, but January is best. If you get it right, it makes a huge difference to the year's grass growth. Getting it right is not so easy. You don't need to be spreading it when you have chickens in (airborne diseases) so there's just a week when the sheds are empty. We managed about half the farm last winter when the spreader broke down, and the difference is dramatic. Just one more job that we have to get right next time.

By the time you read this, milk advertising will be well under way. Apparently it will feature well-known milk drinkers like George Best. I still have reservations about this because of the steady drip of food scare stories that keep surfacing.

I met a man once (who was well placed at Westminster) who told me that animal welfare/vegetarian societies had, collectively, about £30 million to feed these scare stories into the system. That is the scale of the challenge. The latest one in our newspaper tries to link breast cancer to dairy products. Not proven - just someone's theory. Someone told me that under-arm deodorants could cause breast cancer as well.

I should be alright then.

August 2000

Easy Rider

Now is this fair? I had two bank managers in the yard one day, then the dairy inspector turned up. I think the bank managers only came for a laugh so I sent them to look at my neighbour's fields that I told them were mine (better crops), while I showed Stephanie the parlour and dairy.

She's coming again next year, which is just as well, because I don't think she noticed the blue plastic mat I'd bought to stop the tanker pipe chipping the concrete.

My discussions about dogs and quad bikes to fetch the cows have aroused more interest than anything I've written for years. I had five messages on my mobile phone one day:

"I've got a really good cow dog for you (I bet you have) you can have it for nothing (told you)". I declined all these offers. I wouldn't be allowed to get rid of the dog – and we've got too many anyway. But my dog has changed her tactics. She goes as far as the furthest cow and chases it further away. If the furthest cow hasn't got much milk on her I leave them to get on with it.

Strangely, I have not been inundated with offers of free quad bikes, though plenty of people have told me they are essential. David did suggest getting a mountain bike to fetch the cows. Then someone said: "But you'll get cow shit all up your back." So what's new?

No, I have decided there is no need for a quad bike, unless a) the pressure from the grandsons becomes too much or b) I have some spare money. Now, if I had some real spare money I wouldn't buy a quad bike: I'd get a Honda Gold Wing. I'd ride it wearing designer jeans, T-shirt and sunglasses and take it, and my designer belly, off to tour France.

We keep on farming out of habit. I thought the cows were shitting a bit loose this year, until the day I gave them too many potatoes.

We've decided to increase the cows next year. The parlour will stay the same, so all we're really doing is putting our hands up for more work. One thing I have decided for certain is, I won't have any hassle at milking time. For over 30 years my cows have kept me. Now I'm keeping them. Some cows haven't realised the significance of this. With milk prices as low as this you don't need a kicking getting it. One cow has already been banished to the orchard with two calves to suck her. If you stood at one end she'd lick you, if you stood the other she'd kick you. Bollocks to that.

One or two people have suggested I look tanned and asked if I've been on holiday. The truth is our kitchen window fell apart last January. I get weatherbeaten just eating breakfast. We've had a new window frame on the yard for six months now. But as the builder said, there's no rush, as long as it's in before next winter. Which is just what the plumber said last year about the secondhand Rayburn we'd bought and which is still in his shed. It's also roughly what the technicians said about our central heating which broke down at Easter. Laid back! I sometimes think I'm living in southern Ireland, not south Shropshire.

I was a bit dry one morning and had three cups of tea before milking – and guess where some Uddermint ended up? Now that we've got these little boys about (who are showing naturist tendencies) let's just use their wee willie winkie-speak. Anyway, that Uddermint still hurts. I haven't done it for years and I should know better at my age. Then again, any sensation is better than nothing at my age.

I spent two days at the Royal Show. Everyone seems to think the price of milk will shoot up. As I wandered about, I reckoned it went up 1ppl every 35 yards. I also spoke to people who represented every possible point of view of the dairy farming political spectrum. But I detected one common thread: "We must all work together". I like farming people and especially those who milk cows for a living. Sometimes I wish I could reach out and gather them all in my arms – then bang their bloody heads together.

September 2000

Embryonic Entrepreneur

So what's been happening? We have had our local beer festival – something I could well do without. All these real ale buffs wandering about smacking their lips, taking half-an-hour to choose half a pint of beer then taking half-an-hour to drink it. People from places like Hertfordshire and Wolverhampton. Some of them even try to sit in my seat which really pisses me off.

This woman sits down next to me and, as she sips Glenfiddich to take away the taste of beer, she says: "I'm from Milton Keynes, where are you from?"

"Five miles down the road."

"Oh, fairly local then?" She wouldn't go away.

"What do you do for a living?"

"Farmer."

You will have noticed and worked out by the brevity of my replies that she was neither young nor smart.

"Ooh, I've never met a farmer before, I've always wanted to ask this question."

"Go on then."

"Is it right that male pigs have got corkscrew dicks?"

I ask you, why does this sort of thing always happen to me? What sort of question is that to ask a sensitive young boy?

"Yes, it's true, that's where the word screw comes from."

And finally, before I move on to the next part of my task, why, when military aircraft (we're in a low-flying area) can apparently fly with such precision, does every plane that comes over this farm, be it Tornado fighter or the stately procession of five Hercules bombers that we see regularly, fly right over the top of our chicken sheds?

I've been asked to write about what I see myself doing five years from now. I need to get away sometimes. Away from all the phones and all the secretaries. Getting away means a couple of hours on my Honda Goldwing. I'd always promised myself one when I won more than £10m on the lottery.

The past five years have been a whirlwind for me. Things started to improve when the European Court ruled that the MMC 'milk' enquiry was flawed and all Milk Marque members received 5ppl for five years' production. Part of the compensation was to give each of the MM successor co-ops 50 supermarkets. I'm passing an Axis supermarket now. I never go in there.

The 10 top officials from the Department of Trade and Industry and 10 from the Office of Fair Trading were sentenced to 10 years' milking cows for no wages (so they would know what it's like).

I managed to pull a few strings and I got them jobs at the Axis supermarkets collecting trolleys in the car parks. That's why I don't go in there - their gratitude can be a bit embarrassing.

I do keep an eye on what's going on. The price of milk has been more than the price of bottled water for four years now. What really took off for me was my cattle breeding enterprise. A combination of my lottery money, cloning, the very latest development in embryology and my own brilliant mind has enabled me to take a fast-track to the cow of the future, embryos for which I have sole world rights.

I can supply a cow that will give 10,000 litres of milk on five-times-a-week milking, she will do it readily on a diet of nettles, thistles and docks in summer, plastic bags and straw in winter. Not only that – and this was the really tricky bit – she is guaranteed not to shit in the parlour, always to lie in her cubicle and, with a minimum of training, back up to the edge of your slurry pit to empty herself so that you never have to scrape the yards. She will never have a natural calf because if you want another like her you have to buy the embryo off me.

The breeding business is on a roll now, and largely looks after itself, so I am able to devote more time to my other interests. These include coach and team manager of the Welsh rugby team. We haven't lost a game for four years now and are usually so far ahead in the second half that I am able to go on the field myself, including 10 minutes when we won the World Cup final.

It's not been without its controversy. I took the Six Nations tournament back to Five when I refused to let Wales play England last year. I can't let our standards get dragged down to their level.

Hell! That was close. I've had to stop the bike in a hurry. There's a young girl hitchhiking and the driver of the sports car in front has stopped to pick her up. Tall, blonde, elegant, she runs her eye over the sports car, walks past it, and without a word climbs on the bike with me. I put the bike in gear. And the alarm clock goes.

First decision of the day, do I try to get the dream going again (which would make it a fantasy), or do I get up to milk and use the time to have an extra cup of tea?

The tea wins, I can fantasise while I'm milking.